D1626764

THE ADOPTION TRIANGLE

What Children Can Tell Us About Divorce
and Stepfamilies

THE ADOPTION TRIANGLE

Searching and Uniting

JULIA TUGENDHAT

BLOOMSBURY

First published in Great Britain 1992
Copyright © 1992 by Julia Tugendhat
The moral right of the author has been asserted
Bloomsbury Publishing Ltd, 2 Soho Square, London W1V 5DE
A CIP catalogue record for this book
is available from the British Library
ISBN 0 7475 1010 5
10 9 8 7 6 5 4 3 2 1
Phototypeset by Intype, London
Printed in England by Clays Ltd, St Ives plc

IN MEMORY OF LUCIE

CONTENTS

INTRODUCTION

This book came about in an unexpected way. It all started when television producer Sally Doganis decided to make a documentary on people searching for lost family. Her aim was to interview people who were trying to trace members of their family with a view to reuniting with them. In fact the programme was never made but the BBC went as far to broadcast a Ceefax appeal for people who were looking for parents, siblings, or children to make contact. The response was totally unexpected. Sally was overwhelmed by a flood of emotional and moving letters from correspondents.

Many wrote long letters containing their life histories. One married woman of fifty-seven ended hers with these poignant words: 'I will understand if you can't help, but all my life I have hoped and dreamed of meeting my brother. Yours living in hope.' A man of fifty-three who was adopted at the age of three wrote: 'I am not in such great health myself, but would love to know if I still have a blood relative at all. I did write to Cilla Black but wasn't one of the lucky ones.' Another man wrote in with the few meagre details he had with the plea: 'I would dearly love to know if my parents are alive; if not, at least a brother or sister.' These few words from a married woman of thirty-two speak volumes: 'I'm looking for my real mother – my adoptive mother is now dead. I was in a children's home for eleven weeks before I was adopted through the courts. I've wanted to meet my mother for a long time – I want to find out the reasons why she gave me away.'

Sally Doganis urged me to write a much-needed book on searching in order to reach out to 'the hundreds of people out there who are desperate for advice, information and support.' With very little hesitation I took up the challenge. Since then I have had many misgivings. I have often felt inadequate to the task because I am neither an adoptive parent, a relinquishing parent or an adopted person. I have tried to put myself in the shoes of all the people I interviewed but knowledge and understanding is not the same as experience, though my detachment as an outsider may have been useful in seeing the whole picture. I also felt at times that I had bitten off more than I could chew, especially as there are so many experts in the adoption field who know more than I do. I have relied heavily on their guidance, information, and encouragement to produce a readable book accessible to the layperson.

And of course I have been daunted by the complexity of the subject. Searching contains many elements. It can simply be a quest for information, in itself a complicated process. Or it can lead on to the tracing of family members which in turn can lead to reunions in all sorts of different shapes and sizes. I made a common mistake at the beginning which was to concentrate on one side of the adoption triangle – the adoptees, because they are the ones who usually initiate the search. It didn't take me long to realise that the other sides of the triangle – the birth parents and the adoptive parents – were equally important.

So more and more pieces of the puzzle kept popping up. I needed help to sort them out and advertised for anyone who had been involved in searching or reunions (whatever the outcome) to get in touch with me. The response was heartening. I managed to interview or correspond with the majority of those who contacted me. I am indebted to the twenty-six men and women who shared their intimate stories with me. Even though I only use a few of the interviews in full, I learnt something useful from each one.

I became instantly aware of the enormous sensitivity felt by the parties involved in searching and reuniting. Adoptees have lost the parents who gave them life; in many cases adoptive parents have lost the chance of having their own children, only to fear losing their adopted ones, and the birth parents have lost the children they brought into the world. Adoption is a unique blend of gains and losses, great joy and intense pain, but the pain and loss is a reality that is less often acknowledged.

Responding to the wishes of my interviewees who were anxious to avoid hurting others, I guaranteed to disguise names and identifying features. Delicate handling is also needed for the tricky subject of terminology: for example, adopters are sensitive about the adjective 'real'. The adoptee quoted above used the word to describe her birth mother. Does this make the adoptive mother who nurtured her and brought her up any less real? Mothers who gave birth often refer to themselves as the 'natural' mothers, which by implication makes the adoptive mothers feel they are unnatural, whereas the term 'biologic mother', often used by Americans, has clinical overtones. Birth mother and father seem to be the least emotive ways of referring to the original parents. Birth parents are sensitive about the phrase 'to give a child up for adoption' as this seems to imply a voluntary action. I prefer to use the words 'relinquish' or 'placed for adoption', which sound more neutral. Even the ordering of my chapters gave me pause for thought. When addressing the different perspectives, whose should I put first? I decided to deal with the cast in the order of appearance on the scene: the birth parents, the children, and the parents who adopted them.

For searches and reunions to be properly understood, they must be placed in the wider context of a rapidly changing adoption scene. During the last fifteen years or so a fresh breeze of openness has been sweeping away the cobwebs of secrecy that shrouded adoption. When legal adoption was introduced in England and Wales in 1926 and in Scotland in 1930, professional opinion considered secrecy to be in the best interests of everyone involved in the adoption triangle. It was thought that the less adoptees knew about their origins the better, so that the child's links with its genetic past were cut off and he or she was given a brand new identity, with a new name and new birth certificate. This was partly done to protect the birth parents from the social stigma of having produced children out of wedlock, but it was mostly done to protect the adoptive parents. Adoption was primarily seen as a service to childless couples.

But as time went on this policy of concealment came under attack as experts began to acknowledge that it was not in the best interests of adoptees to be cut off from their past. Following the gradual revelation of the confusion and bewilderment adoptees suffered from being severed from their genetic roots, the law was changed in 1975 to enable them to have access to their original birth certificates and ultimately, therefore, to original family members. It is interesting to note that in Scotland adopted people of seventeen have always had the right of access to their original birth certificates. The National Organisation for the Counselling of Adoptees and Parents (NORCAP) was founded in 1982 to assist those involved in searching.

Since 1975 immense changes have been taking place, shifting the emphasis from adoption being a service for childless couples to a service for children needing families, and bringing a spirit of openness in their wake. The main reason that the pattern of adoption has changed is because the number of babies available for adoption has dropped drastically to less than twenty per cent of the 7,000 children adopted in England and Wales. Contraception, changing attitudes to illegitimacy, and housing for single parents have contributed to the diminution. At the same time there has been an increase in the number of infertile people. Adoption agencies have responded to this change by encouraging families to adopt children with special needs – older children who have been in care, siblings, and children with emotional or physical disabilities. The enthusiastic and creative campaign to find homes for hard-to-place children has been very successful. Parent to Parent Information on Adoption Services (PPIAS), which was founded in 1971 as a voluntary self-help group, has been particularly supportive to such families.

Openness and honesty are essential ingredients in the adoption of children with special needs. When children are taken out of care or foster homes and placed for adoption at any age from one to eighteen there can be no hiding of past history. The children have an identifiable past that they can remember and are encouraged to remember by social workers who help them to make life story books of the family members they have known, the hospital they were born in, and the homes and schools they have attended. If it is appropriate they might still have some contact with parents, grandparents, or other relatives.

Transracial adoption has also reinforced the spirit of openness. Although agencies nowadays aim to place black or mixed-race children wherever possible with same-race families, transracial adoption flourished between the mid-Sixties and mid-Seventies. When children are a different race from their adoptive family, it is impossible to hide their origins. Furthermore, there has been a growing awareness that these children need to identify with their ethnic roots and culture.

The openness inherent in transracial adoption and the adoption of children with special needs has inevitably had an impact on the traditional closed adoption policy. In the USA and New Zealand the door is being opened to allow a more co-operative model of adoption.

The door can be opened in varying degrees, from partly open, with birth parents being involved in the selection of adoptive parents, to wide open, when an arrangement is made for ongoing contact between adoptive and birth parents. Somewhere in between there can be arrangements for non-identifying one-off meetings, and a regular exchange of information and photographs through the agencies.

These changes have come about because, with the scarcity of babies for adoption, birth parents and especially birth mothers have been able to express their needs and wishes more forcibly. The balance of power in the adoption triangle has shifted in their favour. They feel empowered as never before to have their say in both the open adoption and the reunion debate. In Britain birth parents now have their own support group. The Natural Parents' Support Group (NPSG) was formed in 1987, thus bringing the last side of the triangle into the frame alongside PPIAS and NORCAP. The government is planning to overhaul adoption procedures in 1992 to bring the law into line with the trends and changes that have been taking place on the ground. I shall be discussing these in the last chapter when I look towards the future.

Because adoption is such an enormous and complex subject I have had to set myself strict parameters. For instance, I do not deal with the large number of adoptions within the family, mostly by step-parents, which accounts for more than half of the 7,000 adoptions a year in England and Wales. Nor do I include the vast number of children who were removed from British orphanages and institutions before and after World War

II and sent abroad to Canada and Australia. Not only did these individuals often lead a life of hardship and misery, but their records and papers were destroyed so they reached adulthood without roots and a sense of identity. Many of these children, who are now middle-aged or old, have spent years trying to trace their families over here. Thanks to the Child Migrants Trust, set up by Margaret Humphreys in 1987, some families have been reunited.

I consider that children adopted from countries like India, South America, Lebanon, and Romania are in a special category of their own too. Transcountry adoptions have many features in common with transracial adoptions. The adoptees may feel a need to identify with their lost families and countries, but being victims of poverty, social upheaval, or war, searching as such will not be a practical option for them. They will need help to create a sense of identity for themselves from other sources within the adoptive community.

There are about three-quarters of a million adopted people in England and Wales. I have restricted myself to those, adopted in the closed model, who are involved in searches and reunions. It is impossible to be precise about numbers but guesstimates range from twenty per cent to NORCAP's suggestion that thirty-one per cent of adopted men and fifty-nine per cent of women make enquiries into their backgrounds. Then there are the other people in the triangle – members of the adoptive and birth families – who become involved. This book is written for children, parents, grandparents, brothers, sisters, relatives and friends who want to know more

INTRODUCTION

about searches and reunions from the ordinary people
who have experienced them.

THE BIRTH MOTHER

I know a great many adopted children, but before embarking on this book I don't believe I had ever given a thought to the mothers who brought them into the world. Quite unconsciously I had joined in the general conspiracy to treat birth mothers as if they were invisible. Since the Adoption Act of 1926, about three-quarters of a million mothers parted with a child for adoption in Britain. During this time society, professionals, families, and adopters made a tacit pact to ignore their existence.

These mothers, mostly very young and who bore children out of wedlock, were made to feel like sinners and transgressors who should be grateful to the childless couples eagerly awaiting their 'unwanted' babies. Many of them were banished from their homes and families to have their babies alone, believing that relinquishment was the only course open to them. They had almost no say in the choice of the parents who were to adopt their babies, and signed over for eternity their rights as mothers to nameless people about whom they knew virtually nothing. They did not expect ever to have news of their children again. They were then told by everyone involved to go home and forget what had happened. Many of them never mentioned the subject again.

But when the 1975 Children Act gave adult adoptees access to their original birth certificates the position of birth mothers was radically altered. Media coverage being what it is, there must now be very few of them who would be taken by surprise if they were to be contacted by the children they thought they had lost for ever. When they see reunions emotively orchestrated on television by Cilla Black and Kilroy, or realistically enacted in *East Enders*, they will be aware that the social stigma surrounding illegitimacy has all but disappeared.

Nevertheless, it seems that some birth mothers dread being found and refuse contact. There are many and complex reasons why a birth mother might feel this way. Having surrendered her child she might feel she has no right to have further contact. She is likely to be older and more old-fashioned. The chances are that no one in her present family knows about the child she relinquished and she is frightened of being judged by family and friends. Perhaps her parents who had insisted on the adoption are still alive. Having denied the existence of the child for so long she may feel she cannot cope with the emotions that a reunion would stir up. She might still be feeling hurt and angry with the child's father. Expecting to be blamed for what she did, she may fear rejection by her son or daughter. She may dread being faced with the truth – learning, perhaps, that her child had an unhappy adoptive experience. Or she may fear that her child has led a better life and will look down on her.

The majority of birth mothers probably wait and see what fate will bring with a mixture of longing and trepidation. The co-ordinater of the Natural Parents' Support Group told me, 'There is not one mother in touch with us who doesn't want her child to find her, but there are obviously thousands who are not in touch.' When the NPSG first got the BBC's *Open Space* programme to give them a chance to go public, they were flooded with enquiries and appeals for support. They reply to every letter they receive and send out a regular newsletter.

And then there are the birth mothers who are simply longing to be found. They can take matters into their hands only as far as leaving their details and current addresses with the General Registrar at Titchfield, NORCAP and the original adoption agency in case their children start looking for them. Some of these birth mothers are going public and saying this is not enough. They are pressing for legislation to be changed so that mothers have a right to identifying information when their children come of age, just as they do in New Zealand.

They argue that just as adoptees need to know where they come from, birth mothers need to know what has happened to the children they brought into the world. They feel it is unjust that women who placed their babies for adoption at a time when sex education, birth control, abortion and state benefits were not available should feel compelled to act as if times have not changed. Why should they continue to be punished in today's more enlightened social climate? They want to know if their children are alive, well and happy. They have no wish to behave irresponsibly towards the adoptive parents or to disrupt their children's lives. What makes them sad and angry is if they find that the adoptive parents split up, or died, or the children went into care when they might have been in a position to offer them a home.

Agency responses to pressure from birth mothers are sympathetic but cautious. According to Phillida Sawbridge of The Post-Adoption Centre (PAC), 'Although the law is silent on the question of birth mothers searching, the centre does not help them to find lost children. We tell them that their children may not know they are adopted or may not be ready. But the centre would like to know more about the outcome of reunions in which the mother has initiated the search.'

'I personally feel that the situation is inequable as it is,' admitted Pam Hodgkins of NORCAP. 'We can change most of the big decisions in our lives such as jobs and partners. It isn't fair that people who made decisions when they were young should live with that for ever and ever. Also, I know that many people have the information to search effectively anyway. Within a limited way we've been assisting, though it is not a policy decision in our organisation.'

As far as birth mothers are concerned there is a huge gap needing to be filled. There are few books they can read to help them make sense of their feelings; no research; no advice on how to tell subsequent children that they have a brother or sister, or future partners of their history. The following account by a birth mother called Nancy, who spoke to me with palpable emotion and honesty, goes some way to filling the gap.

'*I was nineteen and a student when I got pregnant. I can't say my parents literally sent me away but the atmosphere would have been so dreadful I didn't really have a choice. I knew adoption was the only option, as I knew the sun would come up in the morning. The script was written and I just followed the script. The atmosphere in the Mother and Baby home I went to was bizarre, but I didn't question anything because I actually believed that I was so bad that it was the right way to treat me. None of us rebelled against it. It was part of the punishment that we deserved. There were very strict rules and we kept them – it was part of being an unmarried mother at that time.*

'*There was a male doctor attached to the home and part of the ethos of the place was that he didn't speak to you. He gave you the most intimate examination in silence as if you didn't exist. He would say to the midwife, "Tell her to bend her knees. Tell her . . ." That was one of the worst memories I've got. It felt very invasive. For all of us it was our first labour and it was terrifying to be in that situation because you didn't know how you were going to be treated or what was going to happen to you. I was in labour for days – it sort of spun on and on. When it got serious I was taken into the lying-in room and left on my own for the first stage of labour. When I started the second stage I had to scream for someone to come from downstairs.*

'It was a very difficult birth because the baby was quite big and three weeks late. They said it was a girl, weighed her and put her in a cot. My whole dream was getting out of that place. Everything was geared in my head to getting back to what I was before, the person I thought my mum and dad cared about. We had to breast-feed for three weeks. Looking back I now recognise that my head was completely cut off from feeling, but I can remember her physically. My body felt her very strongly. Communication with a baby is on such a physical level – the smell of a warm head and a powdery little bottom. I'm really glad that I remember like this.

'Adoptions took place in the adoption agency in town. In my week there were four of us. My mum and dad came for me, and without being asked whether I minded, we were told we had to give a lift to one of the girls who was hysterical in the car going to town. So it ended up with my mum carrying my baby in the front, while I comforted her in the back because I didn't want my father to get angry.

'We were shown into a dark, windowless room divided by a partition with an adjoining door. As I was the fourth I had to watch three go through until it was my turn. The adoptive couple would come into the adjoining room and you could just about hear what they were saying. It reminded me of death row listening for your turn. I was left with

a little girl of fifteen who looked as if she was shell-shocked and didn't move the whole time. The social worker would come through and take the baby next door to give it to the couple. They would then go out of the front door and we would be shown out by the back door which was the tradesman's entrance. I had a grey furry kitten to go with my daughter and when the social worker took her I heard this couple saying to the little girl they had adopted earlier, 'Here's your sister,' and they gave her the kitten.

'I thought, "She's not your sister she's my baby." How could they say that with me next door? I just find it incredible that this adoptive couple could have claimed her as theirs within earshot of me. Maybe they didn't know I was there, but I find it amazing that in such a short distance she was theirs not mine. I feel very angry about the way all that was done. Just in the last year I've felt this anger. I went home with mum and dad who had put me in a new bedroom and redecorated it. It was all new beginnings. My mother even bought me a white dress. I went back to work leaking milk and hoping nobody would notice the wet patches.

'When I got married I got pregnant right away. It was absolutely deliberate – it was doing it properly. I had the wedding ring and I could go to antenatal classes in an ordinary hospital like other women. At the time it was part of me making myself normal, but it wasn't a replacement. Everything about that baby was beautiful. My husband was allowed to be in on the birth. They knew I

had had a baby before, it was obvious, and they asked what the first one was and he said, "Oh, a little girl," without batting an eyelid. His own daughter had just been born and I thought it was amazing. He went off to buy a little grey furry kitten but only managed to find a white one.

'Then she was ill and I had to come home without her and I thought, "She'll die and I won't get to bring the second one home either." It was a feeling of fate. I can remember looking at her in the cot, thinking, "If anyone told me they were going to take you away, I wouldn't just hit them, I'd kill them." I was very anxious for the whole of her first year. Then I got a fixed idea that I wanted to adopt a child. Other birth mothers may tell you the same thing. If I was actually considered good enough to adopt a baby then I would be as good as the people who had taken mine. Eventually I decided to have another child of my own.

'I got pregnant and from that moment I had this doom-laden feeling that something terrible was going to happen. I now see that I had a lot of guilt feelings because I didn't have to tell anyone that I had had two children because all the stretch marks and things could be explained, so I said I only had one. What a shitty thing to do to my first child, I really cut her right out of that pregnancy and I did it consciously because I still wanted to be a good person. I was supposed to have the baby at home, but in the end he was overdue and I was rushed into hospital. As it happens I had a doctor whose use of English was poor so I was examined by *someone who didn't speak to me, in a hospital I had never been to, and I began to get an awful panic feeling. There hadn't been time to fetch my husband. I was put in a side-ward and had to shout for help again. It was such a carbon copy.*

'After the birth I was put in the middle of the ward because there were no empty beds and it was something about being surrounded by all this empty space which finished me. I screamed and screamed and said I was dying, and this sister came with an injection, and I remember saying, "He isn't my second, he's my third," and she said, "It doesn't matter," and I said, "It does matter." When I woke up I didn't think any more about what I'd said. It was as if the injection took it away. I ended up in a psychiatric hospital, feeling I was going mad but nobody attached it to the fact that I had had a child adopted.

'I didn't talk about her again for six years, during which time I was depressed to a greater or minor extent. Eventually I got referred to a psychotherapist and in the first interview he asked how many children I had. To which I replied that I had two: I had had a third but had given it away so it didn't count, and he thought, "this woman needs help." I saw him for over two years and by the end my first child was a she and had a name, and she was the appropriate age, and I was able to tell my other children about her.

'I went back to college and got friendly with a mature student who had come there by the same route as me – through a depression following an

abortion. She was so aware and open about her feelings and I thought how amazing that she allows herself to feel this thing. And I told her about the adoption. A few weeks later I saw an advertisement about a birth mothers' group at the Post-Adoption Centre. I got there early and looked around. There were all these books about adoption, and it sounds dramatic but it was as if my life changed at that moment because I thought, "This is about me. It really is me that did it, not anyone else." I went to the toilet and cried and cried. The group became the most important thing I did every month.

'*I never intended to trace my daughter but then I had a party for some students in college who knew about her because I had become so much more open about telling, and one of them casually asked, "Well aren't you going to find her, then?" I didn't do anything about it until my husband and I went away for a brilliant weekend and everything was perfect and I kept on getting these good vibes. It felt the right time. I wasn't doing anything out of despair but at a happy time in my life. Everything about the search went right. When I found her house I felt that my balance had been restored – being allowed to find her was a message to me that I wasn't the bad person I had thought I was all these years. I've only traced her. Even if I never meet her I will have made this journey in which I changed as I travelled.*'

Although Nancy's experience is unique she touches on issues that will be only too familiar to other birth mothers. They will be able to identify with her terrible feeling of powerlessness after she found she was pregnant. Feeling pressurised for lack of options, acquiescing to the opinions of others, however well meaning, is not a sound basis for making the most significant decision of a lifetime. Even as I write this I feel angry with the do-gooders who allowed an inexperienced, terrified young woman to bear her baby, give birth to it and then relinquish it in such callous and insensitive circumstances.

Today when counselling services are automatically laid on at the scene of major accidents and tragedies, it is difficult to comprehend the mentality which produced the advice 'go home and forget all this ever happened'. What we know now is that it is vital for people undergoing trauma, shock, loss, and tragedy to be able to express their natural feelings of anger, sorrow, guilt, and resentment. Feelings which are repressed or denied will come out in unexpected and inappropriate ways which may never be properly identified or understood.

PAC has published some interesting findings from the group meetings they have been organising for birth mothers. They started the meetings in response to 'the litany of grief, anxiety, confusion, and isolation' expressed by birth mothers. Over 1,200 women have been in touch with the centre in the last three years. It is clear that they feel cheated by the lack of preparation they were given at the time of relinquishment.

They believe that they experience a bereavement which cannot be resolved because there has not been a death or the rituals that accompany death. Being told to try and forget and that the pain would go away was not helpful. They felt they could have coped much better if they had had a more honest and realistic picture of the pain that never goes away. If only they had been able to prepare to encounter remarks such as 'Only a selfish woman could give up a child,' or 'How many children do you have?' If only they had been warned of the triggers such as a child's birthday or a death in the family, or a programme on television that would unexpectedly churn up emotions.

An Australian study of relinquishing mothers has revealed that birth mothers are more likely to suffer from illness and nervous disorders than the rest of the population. This appears to be the result of repressed mourning and the consequences of living with un-resolved stress. Not all birth mothers have the same reactions, but some of the difficulties experienced by Nancy may ring a bell. She suffered from postnatal depression and nervous breakdowns. Her relationship with her parents deteriorated because of the resentment she felt towards them. For years and years she was tortured by feelings of guilt and low self-esteem. She tried to obliterate her baby from her memory and only succeeded in freezing it in time.

The rewards Nancy has received from her intense struggle to understand her loss have been liberating. When she and her daughter meet she and her family will be ready for it. But not every birth mother possesses her resources or self-awareness. That is why it is impor-tant for someone like Nancy to be able to articulate their concerns. If adoptees and adopters can understand something of what birth mothers might have experi-enced, and try to put themselves in their shoes for a

moment, they will be better prepared for handling reunions.

THE BIRTH FATHER

While the birth mother is becoming more visible in the reunion process, the birth father is still a shadowy figure. Yet he too helped to create a child who might, in the course of time, seek him out. The Post-Adoption Centre believes that fathers have many of the same needs as birth mothers, but very few make contact and none come to the group meetings. Likewise, Margaret Humphreys finds that men do not join her Triangle group but may seek advice on the telephone. 'There is more awareness about men in adoption now than there has been in the past. My experience is that men go through feelings in relation to guilt similar to those of natural mothers, but it isn't socially acceptable for men to come forward. If they contact me it is probable that they have been thinking about it a lot.' The Natural Parents' Support Group also finds that enquiries come almost exclusively from mothers. When I advertised for interviewees from all parties involved in reunions only one birth father responded.

Betty Jean Lifton, author of *Lost and Found*, calls the quest for the father the Mini-Search. This is because in her experience adoptees generally look for their fathers after they have absorbed the reunion with their birth mothers. They may do it quickly or take years over it. They may look at the search as the last piece of the puzzle, or they may be hoping for a better outcome if the reunion with the mother has not been satisfactory.

In any event many more reunions take place with mothers and siblings than with fathers. This is because for many adoptees, finding the mother is fulfilment enough and they have no need to look further, or they are stopped short in their tracks for lack of information. Unless the birth father has given his consent his name will not be on the original birth certificate. The adoption agency may have details of the father on record but can use its discretion about revealing them. It is very important to adoptees to know that they were not conceived as the result of a casual or callous sexual encounter, and the absence of the birth father's name on the birth certificate often comes as a great disappointment and tends to ring alarm bells. But it is important to remember that the absence of the name does not necessarily mean that the adoptee was conceived as a result of rape or a one-night stand, or that the father did not care. The fathers (often as young as the mothers) could have been subject to the same social and family pressures. Some of them may not have been told of the pregnancy and birth, or given any encouragement to offer support.

Unless an adoptee has access to a name, he or she will be dependent on the mother for information. It might be very difficult to get details from a mother who is still feeling hurt, bitter or humiliated. She might refuse to talk about the father or paint a picture that is off-putting. Notwithstanding the difficulties in the way of tracking down birth fathers, Pam Hodgkins finds it surprising that so few are involved in reunions. 'Do adoptees see him as of less importance?' she asks. 'Is he less responsible? Why are some agencies unwilling to name fathers even if they acknowledged the child and contributed to its maintenance? Why do so few birth mothers assist or encourage the search for the father?' She considers that the answers to these questions are contained in the very heart of our acceptance of the relative positions of men and women in society.

Several of the adoptees I interviewed had access to their father's name and address but considered that contact would be likely to cause unjustified disruption. Their premise was that the present families of their fathers were unlikely to know anything about the past and so it was better to let sleeping dogs lie. This seems to me to be a sensible presumption. Fathering a child does not leave identifying scars. Men can get away with denying paternity and often do. Lifton describes her own father as the type who used to be called a bounder or a cad: 'I see my macho father and his type in the chimpanzee male who, having had his sport, is off to other parts of the forest.'

One young man I interviewed gave me an extraordinary account of meeting his father who had been an American serviceman. After tracing and corresponding with him he went to meet him in the United States. 'He was pretty surprised,' Peter told me, 'but he figured that someone had to turn up sooner or later because there were quite a few of us. While I was actually staying with him there was a phone call in the middle of the night. It was from another one from England who had spent seven years trying to find him. All hell broke loose. He had been posted everywhere. I said, "Come on, there's got to be some more around." We've found out there's another in Europe. I've got siblings all over the globe. I feel a bit sorry for my father.' This is a perfect example of Lifton's 'macho' father who had misspent his youth indiscriminately spreading his seed around. But at least he did not deny that he was Peter's father.

Even if a man has not told his present wife or family about the child he fathered many years earlier, he is not necessarily going to reject that child if he is contacted. I was struck by the fact that three adoptees told me that the reactions of their fathers had been resigned, if not relieved at being found. Knowing full well that the law had been changed in 1975, it was as if they were waiting for their numbers to come up. A father's attitude is likely to depend on his former feelings for the mother. If he felt good about her his response is likely to be positive. But if he had been ignored or bullied by her family, his response may be negative. The best outcome is if the parents subsequently got married, which happens quite often. The following story is told by Nick, the only father who volunteered for interview. He is a young-looking man of fifty with an outgoing personality.

'My daughter was born as a result of teenage first love. There was nothing nasty about it. Pat and I lived two miles apart – she in a nice housing estate, and me on the local council estate. We went to the same nursery and then the same school. She was in the class below me. The friendship started because there was a lot of bullying going on and I was protective of her and so a very close friendship developed. I used to walk to and from school with her. I got introduced to her mum and dad and I used to visit regularly. I got on well with her mother but her father was a disciplinarian and was upset that his daughter was knocking about with someone from the council estate.

'Then when I was fifteen I joined the Boys' Service in the army. It was when I came home on one leave that I was sent for – not by the family, but by friends of the family, who told me that the baby had been born. I was sixteen and didn't even know that Pat had got pregnant. We were both very innocent and it hadn't crossed my mind that she could get pregnant. Pat had been sent away to the country to live with friends. The baby had come and gone, and nobody knew about it. She went back to another school. I was very upset for her and tried to see her but wasn't allowed to. I was so upset I kept going absent without leave and so was discharged from the army. I told my mother the day I knew I was a father. We always kept that between us and the rest of the family never knew.

'One day I saw her on a cycle going to church and we renewed our relationship against her parents' wishes. We didn't talk about what had happened – it was something that had been cleared up and was out of the way. I wasn't interested in a sexual relationship but was very much in love with her. It was a difficult time because she was worried about hurting her parents and time and again she would say we shouldn't carry on. I felt that if it hadn't been for this pressure we would be together now though I understand the point of view of her father. When I was eighteen I had to move away to work. We had drifted apart by this time. The next thing I knew was that Pat was getting married to one of my friends. I had lost her and was very upset.

'I always thought of my daughter right from the start. She was part of the girl I loved. I was told the baby had been adopted by a family in London, so London became an important part of my life. I used to visit once or twice a year to look round and I knew she was there somewhere. I wasn't expecting to meet her but wanted to be there where she was nearer. I didn't think about my right to be consulted until much later. When I got married I told my wife about my daughter Tina right from the start. When we had our own daughter Fanny I thought about my first child a lot but kept these thoughts to myself in case it hurt my wife.

'I began to think about searching in 1976. I asked the Salvation Army to help me but they refused when they learnt she was adopted. Every now and then I would take it up and then drop it. It was ignorance mainly; I didn't know what to do or how to go about it. Then in 1989 my daughter Fanny was engaged to be married – perhaps that triggered it off. I saw a programme on TV about a lady trying to find her daughter and wrote off to them. They sent me the script and that clinched it for me. NORCAP said they weren't there to help birth parents search but were good enough to print a letter of mine in which I asked for guidance, advice and help to enable me to search for my daughter. The response from birth mothers was amazing. It was a comfort to know there was always someone a phone call away who would listen to me, especially when I was going through times of anxiety and depression.

'I was motivated by my own need to find my daughter, but I also believed that she had a right to know. I thought of the adoptive parents but always in my mind was the knowledge that they had sent a photo of Tina as a baby to the birth mother via a social worker. So I felt that if they were good enough to send the photo they might be sympathetic to what I was doing. I was lucky to get the support of Pat's parents. I wrote to them and was delighted to get a reply saying that they understood. I think they too wanted to know.

'My contact with NORCAP members had persuaded me that it was wrong to go knocking on doors, so when after some lucky breaks I managed to track down Tina's whereabouts I asked a local social worker to act as intermediary. He wrote a letter to her saying a client of his was looking for her. She knew she was adopted and gave the letter to her adoptive parents. Her mum went as white as a sheet and said, "You'd better show it to your father." He said, "Well, that's your original name. That's you." Her mum was very apprehensive, but Tina said, "I don't want to upset you, but I'm going to see." She went into the Social Services with a friend and found out that I was looking for her. She was expecting it to be her mum but found it was her dad. The amazing thing is that she was ready to be found. She had a letter in her handbag before I came on the scene – trying to find her birth mother, but she didn't know where to send it. We were put in contact with each other and spoke on the phone for two hours and met in a hotel the day after.

'She came with her oldest son and asked him to wait outside. He fell asleep in the car and we forgot all about him and went off in my car. I was expecting a replica of Pat to walk through the door and was astonished to find me – she's got a lot of my features. We cuddled each other for five minutes, with all the people milling around, and we had tears in our eyes. At first she called me by my first name, but now says "Dad". She's got two dads and I've got not just her but her whole family.

'I was a bit worried about her adoptive parents so I wrote to them before I was due to meet them. They made me very welcome and we had a cup of tea and a long chat. When I'd left, Tina's mum said to her, "Well, he's met you now and satisfied his curiosity and I don't think you'll meet him again." She thought I might take her away but if anything, us meeting has brought her closer to *them. We're going to meet her grandparents together and they will let Pat know that I've found Tina when they visit her.*

'My own wife has been very supportive even if she has felt uncomfortable about it. I think she said to herself, "Well whatever I say he's going to go and look for her." I was wrong not to tell Fanny about her right from the beginning. I should have been open with her. I think secrets in families are wrong. When I kept going to London to search she knew something was up, so my wife told her what was going on. She's asking a lot of questions and wants to meet Tina. I told my brothers who thought it was hilarious. It's been so much easier to tell people than I ever thought. I've had cards congratulating me on my new daughter. I've got such a nice feeling about it all. I'm really happy to have my daughter. I'm happy she's happy. I'm glad to be there in case she needs me to make amends for what went on in the past. Yet when I say that, I'm not really making amends because she was born into one situation and went into a nice adoptive home – she's had a good life.'

It is clear from Nick's account that as an adolescent father he was under social pressures similar to many birth mothers. He was not given a chance to take any responsibility for the child he had fathered. He obviously would not have been able to marry or support the girl he loved, but he would have felt less helpless if he had been involved. And because his name was not on the original birth certificate he was not allowed by

Tichfield to put his name on the register as an indication that if his daughter was searching he wanted to be found.

He had never forgotten his daughter. She was always there in the back of his mind, in certain places and at significant times – an experience shared by many birth mothers. The triggers that set him off on the actual search are very similar to those described by adoptees: the birth of his daughter, her engagement, a programme on TV.

In thirty-five years the social climate had changed so much that Pat's father, who had been so harsh at the beginning, welcomed Nick's initiative in looking for Tina. No one disapproved of what Nick was doing. He probably could have safely told his brothers years ago, and certainly wishes he had been more open with his daughter who had begun to misconstrue his visits to London. Nick feels that the birth father is a much maligned figure. He suspects that many men feel as he does, especially if their children were lovingly conceived. They may try to forget but he wonders whether they can. 'I get tired of the way pressure groups and the media always refer to birth mothers. I've been very emotional about my daughter and I want people to know that fathers have feelings too.'

THE ADOPTEE

It is difficult for people like myself who have not been adopted to understand why some adoptees feel driven to search. Adoptive parents, who have loved and cared for their children as if they were their own may regard searching as an inexplicable aberration. It isn't easy for adoptees to describe the identity void they experience: some said they felt incomplete, empty or profoundly dissatisfied. Others were able to tell me very clearly what life events triggered off their searches but tended to describe their motivation in vague terms like, 'I just knew I had to do it;' or, 'My curiosity kept driving me on.'

The term 'genealogical bewilderment', coined by a British psychiatrist, goes some way to describing the state of mind that can lead to searching. The adopted child realises very early on that to be chosen or adopted means that he/she was relinquished by others. For Betty Jean Lifton it is only common sense to consider that adoptees have extra difficulties in adolescence 'when we consider that it is hard to know where you are going when you don't know where you come from'. Adoptees often suffer a sense of being and feeling different. Therapists have long been aware that some adopted adults suffer from a sense of rootlessness, and a fear of failure and rejection. Haimes and Timms, who have written a book on searching, talk about the importance of a 'narrative sense of self' in all aspects of life. 'Adoptees want a narrative in order to place themselves in a continuum of their past, present and future, which will account for and explain the possibilities of their lives which underwent a shift, a disjuncture – even a displacement – when they were placed for adoption.'

But why then do some adopted people search for their birth parents and others do not? Early researchers like John Triseliotis considered searching a sign of psychological maladjustment and dissatisfaction with adoptive homes. And there is no doubt that some adoptees search for alternative or substitute relationships because they feel emotionally deprived. But more recent research suggests that searching arises out of a natural and fundamental rather than a deviant psychological process. Is it wrong to want to make better sense of our lives, to struggle for identity, to look for blood relatives? In a recent survey of 181 adopted adults, Pam Hodgkins found that the majority of searching adoptees described their relationships with their adoptive parents as average or better than average. My own interviews accord very much with this view. More people told me about happy adoptive experiences than unhappy ones. Another point worth making is that not searching is more likely to imply a sense of loyalty than a lack of curiosity.

What all the experts do agree on is that most adoptees

who search do not feel that they received enough satisfying information about their origins from their adoptive parents. Owing to the underlying secrecy, many adoptive parents simply were not given the information to pass on in the first place. But even adoptees who have been given an honest account of their origins will eventually need a visual or mental picture of the couple who gave them life, as well as an understanding of why they were relinquished.

It is also clear that many adoptees find it difficult to talk to their adoptive parents about their adoption. Adoptive parents are sometimes reluctant to impart known information if it is negative for fear of hurting the child. In turn, adoptees are reluctant to ask questions because they sense their parents' insecurities and discomfort in these areas, so over time the subject becomes mutually taboo. When children stop asking questions parents often think it is because they are no longer troubled or curious about their origins, but the reverse is probably true. The irony is that while the child's need to know about his identity grows, the parents are less and less inclined to be reminded that the child they love and nurture was not born to them.

This question of 'telling' is a vexed one. Experts continue to argue over the appropriate age for children to be told they are adopted. Phillida Sawbridge of PAC says that the problem most frequently brought to the Centre is about 'telling – what, how much, and when'. It seems that the timing is not so important as the quality of the information and the way it is given. She stresses that the information needs to be given not once but many times because as the child grows older, he or she develops a greater capacity for understanding and will need more issues explained.

The majority of adoptees search between the ages of eighteen and forty, many waiting until one or both of their adoptive parents have died. Nicky Salway, a counsellor at St Catherine's House, told me that she didn't see many eighteen year olds and was glad about that. 'I don't discourage them but I think it's too young. They may still be having adolescent difficulties with their parents. I always tell older people who fear they may have left it too late that they can probably cope with it better now. Nearly everyone I see is sensible. They have no wish to cause trouble and are prepared to think it through.'

Why more women than men search can only be a matter of conjecture. The trigger points which start people searching are similar for both sexes. It may be a significant birthday, marriage, the birth of a child, some media item, or the need for medical history. Perhaps the difference is due to social attitudes. We still think it is more permissible for women to show their emotions.

I have chosen two contrasting accounts to illustrate the adoptee perspective. The first is told by a woman who had a miserable adoptive experience, the second by a man who was brought up in a happy and secure home.

Clare is twenty-six and unmarried, though she has a steady boyfriend. She is a tiny, vivacious, bird-like creature who speaks with great emotional intensity, verging between laughter and tears. Her chaotic little house is filled with birds, fish, stray cats and a dog.

'*I always knew I was adopted. One of the reasons why I was told was because I was adopted by a single lady, which was very unusual. Obviously she was a Miss and I think it was very hard in those days to sort of explain why I was there. When I started school I realised that I was different from everyone else. When I went back and asked, "Why haven't I got a father?" she said my real mother died shortly after I was born and my father couldn't look after me so I was put up for adoption. I accepted what she had told me as you do at that age, but I started to question things when I got to be a teenager. I went through a hell of a lot of bullying at school. I used to be very distraught a lot of the time because kids used to come up to me and jeer, "I know who your real father is." I used to cry a lot because they teased me so, and I used to think they knew more than I did because I didn't know a lot.*

'*When I began to realise at thirteen that things weren't quite the same as anywhere else I tried talking to my mother but found it difficult. She'd clam up and I didn't like to push because I could see it was hurting and she didn't know that much. She told me that my mother had died of a brain haemorrhage. I was born prematurely at seven months, was very tiny, and wasn't expected to live. "Well," I thought, "one day I'll find my father." I'd have given anything to have had a father coming along to rescue me – a knight in shining armour on a white charger to take me away, and we'd live happily ever after, but obviously he never came. I got to be sixteen and thought, "When I get to eighteen he'll find out and come and get me," but he never did.*

'I discovered boys at fourteen and started to have difficulties with my mum. I was so naïve and didn't know what I was doing. Boys became a big bone of contention between us. It was during an argument we had that I discovered I had two sisters. I suppose I was saying I wished I had a father and brothers and sisters. And this discovery was a big shock to the system. I had these older sisters all of a sudden. All along I had known my real surname but never could remember it. It was a sort of mental block.

'I had quite a difficult time growing up. I got pregnant at seventeen and had to sort it out by myself. I've always been bad with men – men who hit me and things. Whether I can blame it on growing up without a father, or whether my mum wasn't very good with men, being a Miss, or whether it was because I was adopted, I don't know, but the fact is that I'm here and I've got by. My adoptive mum gave up everything for me and did her best. I see that now.

'All the time, searching was in the back of my mind. My father hadn't found me and I hadn't heard from my so-called sisters. I got to be twenty-six and was feeling more stable. I have this boy who's lovely and kind and nice to me, and a house of my own. At eighteen I wouldn't have known what I was doing. But this New Year I made a resolution: "This is the year I'll do something *about it." And when I decide something, I do it.*

'I thought, "If my mother's died, surely they'll have a record of it, so I sent off for a death certificate." Then I thought, "There must be a grave," so I rang up the cemetery. I was told she was aged thirty – poor thing, my heart went out to her. She was divorced which I didn't know and was buried in a public grave. That really got to me. What's a public grave? It's when people can't afford a proper grave. Oh, I was so upset. I thought, "Poor thing, shoved in with everyone else. This is my mother here." I was really, really upset, and I was crying. And what does this divorce mean? When I was being bullied at school they would say, "Your mother's a prostitute, nobody wanted you." Children are so cruel. This brought up what I had felt at school. You think the worst, there is no way you don't. Was she a prostitute? Why did she get divorced? I went through all the possibilities. My mind was going wild.

'Then I got the certificate from the hospital saying she had been dead on arrival from an overdose administered whilst the balance of her mind was temporarily disturbed. I absolutely broke down. It was horrible, horrible. I thought, "Poor thing, she was only thirty," and I'm coming up to thirty. I understand people being at their wits' end. I've been at my wits' end many times when I've had to cope with things. But why my mum when she should have been happy to look after me? Why, why, why? There were endless questions I was getting no answer for. Do I want to know? No I* *don't. Yes I do; I've got to know what is going on. So I thought, "I've got sisters, I'm going to find them." '*

I shall recount how Clare went on to find her sisters in a later chapter. It was a very positive reunion and she was able to fill in the puzzle of her past life to her satisfaction. But so much of her early suffering could have been avoided if she had been told the truth in the first place. She did not feel secure as she grew up and suffered greatly from a sense that her situation was odd. All children fantasise about their birth parents, especially if they have no details to fix on, but Clare's fantasies about her father could not possibly be fulfilled. Her expectations might not have been so unrealistic if she had known even a few facts about his occupation or situation. After all, he would never be a knight in shining armour who was going to rescue her. As she said, you always presume the worst. She presumed that her mother had been a prostitute which was as bad, if not worse, as knowing she had committed suicide because she was depressed.

The difficulty of imparting knowledge like this to a child at an appropriate age cannot be underestimated. Clare's adoptive mother can hardly be blamed for not knowing how best to do it, but it is a pity that she did not receive advice from a social worker. Even if she had been in possession of the true facts, Clare probably would have wanted to search, but she would have been spared the terrible shocks that came her way.

Clare chose her time to search by trusting her instinct. She somehow knew when she was stable enough to do it. I was struck by how many of my interviewees seemed to know when the right moment had come. Clare obviously has a lot of personal problems to work through but her search has steadied her and helped rather than hindered her relationship with her adoptive mother. She says, 'I worry because I see a lot of my mother in me – the way she was with men. I get frightened when I think, "Am I strong enough? Am I going to kill myself?" Then I think, "I've got to do better than my mother so that I can say her life has not been in vain." The questions are endless and are still there but I've got satisfaction from what I've done.'

Nigel's experience was very different from Clare's but he too felt a need to search. A successful actor, he lives alone in a neat and tidy flat in the heart of London.

'I learnt I was adopted when I was five and my mother was pregnant with my sister. She told me that I hadn't come out of her tummy like this new baby; I had been especially chosen. A few years later I was shown my birth certificate with my natural mother's name and place of birth. I knew where it was and used to look at it from time to time. I was told that my mother was young when she had me. I was born in a small village and because of the social stigma she couldn't keep me. The issue was openly talked about and I never felt uncomfortable about asking about it. We even used to go for holidays to the place where I was born. I always felt wanted and had much love and atten-

tion lavished on me, maybe more than on my brother and sister.

'I grew awkward in adolescence when I realised that I had a different identity. I looked so different from the others and began to wonder what my natural mother and father were like. Did I have brothers and sisters who looked like me? I became more difficult and can remember a terrible incident when my father told me off severely. I said he had no right because he wasn't my father. I saw him wilt, he was terribly hurt. I realised I had truly hurt him and from that moment I tried hard to be a good son.

'When I was older I went to a seance with school friends. There was a Chinese medium and we sat round a table and asked if there was a message for anyone in the room. The initials I had been given at birth were pointed out by the glass. That must have rekindled something because no one in the room knew my initials. My parents said that if I wanted to know more they would help me find out. They said I had a right to know, but I wasn't that interested.

'I did nothing about it for years and years. My career filled my days and I didn't feel an emotional need to do it. But when I was thirty-four I went to a relaxation therapist to learn how to cope with stress after a difficult period at work. Talking with her, it transpired that I suffered from a fear of rejection in my emotional and social life which stemmed from being adopted, which was understandable. Something was triggered off and I *decided to search. I had got to the stage when I needed to know who I was biologically, for myself, by myself.*

'I didn't confide in my family. My father had died; I didn't think my brother and sister would understand, and I felt it might be painful for my mother. It was difficult not to tell her because we are so close. I felt as if I was leading a double life and twice I came close to telling her.'

Like Clare, Nigel discovered from the records that his mother had died which was a bad blow but he went on to trace a half-sister, and other members of his birth family. He corresponds regularly with his new family and sees them about twice a year. 'I don't feel the search has radically changed my life but I feel stronger and better off for having gone through it. I know who I am and I can see a family likeness in my sister and myself. I think it has been positive for her too because she was an only child. I've also learnt about my natural mother – what she looked like, and what made her tick. What is curious is that my two mothers are so similar – very loving and understanding. I had nothing to forgive my mother for. I couldn't have had my career if I had been living in a remote village. I understand the reasons why she gave me up and am only sad that she couldn't forgive herself.'

Adopted adults who reunite with birth families have to make their own decisions about whether to tell their adoptive parents or not. Some parents, especially if elderly, may never be able to understand, but adoptees are sometimes more sensitive than they need be. In

Nigel's case it sounds as if it is more of a problem for him than his mother. She has always been open with him and surely, from his description of her, would have supported him. With every year that elapses it will be more difficult to tell her.

I hope it will be clear to adoptive parents who read these stories, as it has been clear to me, that Nigel and Clare were not being deviant or disloyal to their adoptive parents when they embarked on their searches. From very different positions, they both felt they had identity problems and needed to search for their psychological well-being. And both of them found self-healing in the process. If adoptive parents can appreciate the reasons, and take comfort from the results, perhaps they will feel less threatened by the searches.

THE ADOPTIVE PARENTS

Of all the people I talked to for my book, adoptive parents were the most defensive. The only ones who volunteered for interview were those who were enthusiastic about reunions. When I brought the subject up with friends who have adopted children I usually got a clear message that the subject was unwelcome. Frissons of fear were in the air. They felt terribly threatened. That adoptive parents are thrown on the defensive is not surprising. They are the nurturing, ever-present parents. They are the ones who have been there when their children were ill, and through all the significant stages in their lives. They are the ones who have shared in their children's triumphs and pains. And as searching and reunions become more widespread and public, they are now being asked to consider the original parents.

The changes in the philosophy and practice of adoption leave some adopters feeling confused and angry. It is as if the goal posts keep getting moved. In the past, adopters believed that having told their children they were adopted, they were to behave as if those children were born to them. Then they were told to acknowledge their children's pasts and origins. Now there is a lot of talk about more openness in adoption. Does this mean the goal posts are going to be moved again? When adopters hear that in the USA some 'open' adoptions are taking place when birth parents are given right of access to the children they place for adoption, they begin to worry about their own situation. One adoptive mother put it like this: 'Sometimes the changes seem almost a matter of fads, like in fashion or food. The trouble with new moves is that it makes adopters doubt whether they've been doing the right thing. They can very easily get to feel undermined.'

As far as searching is concerned, adoptive parents fall roughly into three categories. There are those who are prepared for their children to search, who tolerate the idea of reunion or even encourage it. This is not to say that they will be immune from the normal emotions of apprehension and jealousy, but they will understand. What they will understand is that the search is not a reflection on their parenting or on them, but a natural need in their children to find out who they are.

Parents who can take a positive view of the search are the ones who have always thought of their adoptive family, not as a second best but as a different sort of family. They acknowledge that their families have unique characteristics. They accept that their adopted children have concerns and difficulties on top of the normal ones, and that people outside the family have different responses to them. If they adopted because they could not have children of their own, they have come to terms with this and have not forgotten the other parents out there who are responsible for their children's existence. They have been able to talk to their children about these parents. And if their children want to search, they will want to be there for them in the turbulent and emotional time ahead. In this way they involve themselves in what is probably one of the most important journeys their children will ever take.

At the other extreme are the parents who have closed the door so firmly on the past that the search, if it comes in their lifetime, is an unbearable shock. They cannot envisage sharing their children with anyone else and are terrified of losing them to these others. They take the search as a personal indictment of their parenting and begin to doubt both the past and the future. They ask themselves how they failed to be good parents; how years and years of nurture and love have meant nothing. If given the choice, they would probably rather not know if their children are searching. In every way the children they adopted have become the children they could not have. Having told them they were 'chosen' they have found it difficult to broach the subject again. When describing the adoption they may have been economical with the truth, or they may have painted an unsympathetic picture of the birth parents. The search throws their infertility back in their faces and they experience again the sense of guilt, shame and loss of this time. The birth parents they pretended were dead have come alive to haunt them.

Somewhere in the middle are the adoptive parents who are aware of the possibility of a reunion but hope it will not come their way. This is an understandable attitude. Being adoptive parents is difficult enough without added complications. Feelings of insecurity and inadequacy are not new to them. At the beginning they may have spent frustrating and humiliating years trying to conceive children of their own. They have had to undergo a unique process of scrutiny and assessment before they are allowed to become parents. A sense of being on trial is combined with doubts as to their entitlement to someone else's child. No wonder they feel they have to be superparents. They have been frequently tested and tried to the limit during the adolescence of their children. Already fragile, their self-confidence is shaken by the knowledge that their adopted children are searching. It is not surprising if parents feel ambivalent about whether they want to be told about searches or not. On the one hand it can be less painful not to know. But, to be excluded from such an important process in their children's lives, especially if they have always been open with each other, can also be painful.

Most children are incredibly aware of their parents' sensitivities and do not want to hurt them, which is why they often wait until one or both of them die before searching. One of the tasks of a birth records counsellor is to try and clarify this issue with the adoptee. Nicky Salway puts it like this: 'I ask if the parents are still alive and whether they know what is going on. I find that the majority of people I see haven't told them. I point out that much depends on how far they intend to go in the search. We may be talking about the next thirty years. I mean, it can be complicated to keep a secret if someone has young children who are visiting one grandmother one Sunday and the other the next.' Pam Hodgkins has a similar view. 'I encourage search-ers to ask themselves whether they are seeking a one-off meeting or a relationship. I ask them to compare their position now with the position their parents were in when they told them they were adopted. It wasn't easy but their parents didn't want them to find out indirectly. Would it not be better that their parents found out from them, rather than finding out by mistake?'

I have chosen three interviews to illustrate varying responses of adopters to their children's searches. Veronica who is forty-eight and married has three daughters – two adopted and one natural. Although the adopted girls are not yet old enough to have access to their original birth certificates, Veronica's attitude to searching is as open and confident as is her attitude to adoption as a whole. She is a warm, sensitive person who made me feel instantly at home.

'We adopted Polly in 1975 and kept her own name as her second name. The agency told us a lot about her mother who wanted to meet us to vet us. It's not too much for a mother to ask for, and I'm so glad we did. First we met Sue's mother, who had come to support her, and then Sue, but not to hand over the baby which would have been too emotional. It was traumatic and we were all in tears. I felt they cared about us. She was happy that we had been chosen and she told us how she had named her daughter after a friend. We feel such love for the natural mother and it is easy for us to give Polly the right feelings about her. We asked the agency how we would tell her she was adopted and they said it would never really arise

if we just brought it in from the beginning, which we did. I still think of her mother. Every milestone Polly passes I feel sad that her mother didn't know and couldn't be proud of her.

'Once when she was doing something appalling and I ticked her off she said, "Well you said last time I did this it wasn't the way you brought me up, so it must be in my genes." I wasn't having this and said, "There is nothing wrong with your genes, so you can't blame it on them." Because I know so much about her family I can say things like that. This word "real" that crops up in adopted families is very important. Polly came back from school one day and said, "Anyway, you're not my real mother." I showed her the defi-nition of mother in the dictionary. A mother is one who gives birth and does the rearing. I said, "In most cases that is the same person, while in your case it is split in two. That doesn't make either of us any less real. Sue was the first and I'm the second."

'The subject of searching hasn't cropped up. She knows she has a right to when she's eighteen, and her mother has written a letter to the adoption society which will be there for her when she comes of age. She's always been open with us so I hope she would be confident enough to tell us if she wanted to.'

Because Veronica has incorporated the existence of the birth parents into her life, she feels no terror at the idea that one day her children might want to meet them, and she will give them all the help she can. She has always been ready to answer their questions and in the case of Polly has been greatly helped by the fact that she met her birth mother and grandmother. The picture she got from this meeting has been a comfort to her and to Polly over the years. Although she would have been opposed to an open adoption involving access while Polly was growing up, she would not have minded sending non-identifying information such as photos if they had been asked for.

Sarah is thirty-seven, and happily married with an only son. She is an only adopted child of parents who shut the door firmly on her past life and therefore reacted very badly to her search.

'My adoptive mum and dad are my parents – there is no question about that. My birth mother has never been a parent to me as they have been, so there is no question in anyone's mind who my parents are. The reason I was adopted was that my adoptive mother had been very unfortunate in having two babies who were born prematurely and died immediately. I'm pleased to say that everything they told me about my adoption turned out to be true, it was just that they did not tell me everything. They operated on a need to know basis. If I asked they would tell me.

'I must have been six years old when I was told I was adopted. It started with my questions about where I came from. My mother didn't want to say that I came from her tummy when I didn't and

that was what made her tell me then. I was in no doubt that I was wanted and am fortunate in having had an almost perfect relationship with my parents. When the law changed in 1975, when I was twenty-four, I remember my mum saying, "You wouldn't want to do that, would you?" and I said, "No, I wouldn't." At the time I meant it. I had been adopted at birth. I must have been happy with that because I never asked more. All my life people have seen photos of me with my parents and commented on the likeness between us. That's how close we are.

'Even after the birth of my son when I became aware that he was my only blood relative I was so busy I didn't give it much thought. It was as he grew up and developed – having so much of me and my husband in him – that I began to wonder about myself. I got my original birth certificate but didn't do anything about it for three years. Then I was in bed with a bad cold and was watching Clare Rayner on TV when NORCAP came up. Without any hesitation I phoned them. They sent me their package and that started me off.

'All through the search I never lied to my parents. I never, for instance, asked them to have my son while I was doing my research, and when I made contact with my birth mother I knew I had to tell them. I couldn't live with such a secret. I had given a lot of thought to how they might react. I never wanted to hurt anyone. I went down with my husband and told them and it was all quite calm. I think they were stunned. My mum got out

the adoption papers which was the day I learnt my father's name. Presuming that it might be disastrous, I had written a letter to them because it is not always easy to say what you want, but because the evening seemed to have gone so well, I didn't give it to them.

'Two days later I got a message from my dad and went down there. If I could have pictured how bad it was it could not have been worse. I learnt that they hadn't slept for two nights. Dad said it was as if they had been thrown on the scrapheap. They could only think of it from their point of view. I could not make them see it was an addition, not a substitution. It was nothing they had done and it had nothing to do with them. At that point I left the letter and it did make the difference. I had put on paper exactly what they needed to know.

'The other way of reassuring them was to agree not to tell my son. I showed them nothing had changed by being the same, by calling in, asking them to babysit, carrying on as normal. All this came naturally but it showed them I meant what I said. We jogged on like this but then I felt the subject was never being mentioned, so when my mum came to sit for a couple of hours I left an old NORCAP newsletter lying around because I thought if she read some of the stories she would have more understanding. Later she was able to ask me if I had met my birth mother yet. When I do, I will be able to tell my mum about the meeting

*and she will see that I have not been looking for
another mother.'*

The first shock for Sarah's parents was having to
acknowledge again after thirty-seven years that they
were not the original parents. As Sarah was their only
child and looked like them, it had been easy for them
to forget her past history. All the insecurities they had
suppressed came flooding back and they felt used as
caretakers. The positive aspect is that Sarah has such a
loving relationship with them that she has ridden the
emotional tempests and feels closer to them than ever.
Meanwhile she is finding out all about her history and
genetic family which makes her feel more complete.

The third account is a good illustration of a more mid-
dling and perhaps more common reaction than the last
two. Pat, aged twenty-nine, and her adoptive parents,
Maggie and Donald, took it in turns to tell me their
story. Pat is the second of two adopted children who
were followed by two natural daughters. There was
much laughter, coming and going of animals, and the
passing round of refreshments in their country house.

Maggie: *When we picked Pat up at three months
old we were told that her mother had done her
best to keep her but the pressures had just been
too much from her family. Telling her she was
adopted came naturally. Before she could understand I told her she was special because I had
chosen her. I glamorised it a little bit in as much*

as I used to say there were a whole lot of little babies and I picked her.

Pat: *But there was only this little scrappy one sitting by itself in the middle of the floor.*

Maggie: *Rubbish! She was a big, fat, bouncy baby.*

Pat: *I don't have any memories of learning I was adopted. I never thought I had a problem. I don't think I ever asked any questions. The only thing I ever worried about was why my birth certificate was different from the normal one. It was a boyfriend who sparked off my search. He said something about my appearance and I said I was adopted. He couldn't believe it. He knows lots of adopted people and told me that girls need to know who their mums are; and I thought, I wonder whether I can. I'd never given it a thought. He knew how to go about it. I didn't tell my parents about it at this stage. I had made up my mind that if I found my mother and she didn't want to know, then why bother anybody. If she did, then I would address that, but I would get the facts first. And if I was going to take a long time I didn't want these two to go through that. In fact, it took three weeks. My birth mother and I spoke on the phone and arranged to meet the next day. She sounded emotional and told me she had been waiting for this phone call for so long. She told me where she lived and I said I knew exactly where it was because I had already been to have a look. She said she would have done the same thing because she's inherently nosy herself. So me and my boyfriend went round there to have dinner with her* and her husband. The two men went down to the pub so we had time on our own. She's my mum and I am fortunate because I have two. If children had been involved it may have been different but as far as I am concerned there's no one else involved so they wouldn't think it funny if I was calling her Mum.

Maggie: *You said to me that when you opened the door it was like looking at yourself.*

Pat: *Yes, I blamed her for my big bum straight away.*

Maggie: *Tell how she had made it easy for you to find her all along the way by keeping her maiden name and leaving information every time she moved. She had no more children.*

Pat: *It was difficult telling Mum and Dad. I told Dad first, and he said, 'Well, go and tell Mum.' So I did. I said, 'I've got something to tell you,' and she said, 'Oh God, you're not pregnant.' She had a gin and tonic pretty quick.*

Maggie: *I was fighting my tears and my stomach was just churning. I suppose initially I felt hurt. You have so many mixed emotions. A bit of hurt, a bit of jealousy and all sorts. As I said to Pat at the time, 'If I had been in your shoes I would have done the same thing.' You do get frightened that she might like her birth mother better than you and that you might not see her again – all these fears go through your head. After she left I was more upset but I didn't want her to see that. When she explained about her birth mother, I thought, 'I've got four children and had the joy of all of*

them, why make life difficult when she can now enjoy Pat when she's missed out on twenty years.
Donald: *My view is that you don't own anyone. Freedom is important to me in all respects whether it's animals or humans. Maggie and I had talked about it. We always thought if anyone would search it would be this one.*
Pat: *I'd like to think I haven't changed at all. What springs to mind first is that there is someone in the world I am really related to. Both families came round and had a meal in my flat.*
Maggie: *I worried about what she would think of us. Would she approve of us as parents, would she like us? When we left she produced a great big bouquet of flowers and a card which said 'Thank you'.*
Maggie: *If Pat got married I assume we would both be invited to the wedding.*
Pat: *I have no intention of getting married.*
Donald: *None of us would be invited. She would probably go off and do it and tell us afterwards!*

The fact that Pat's parents had four children, including two of their own, must have made it easier than Sarah's parents to accept the search. The slightly bland tone of the interview was probably a cover for deeper emotions, but there is no doubting the respect and understanding everyone in this adoption triangle had for the others. The birth mother was grateful, the adoptive parents were generous, and the adoptee incorporated a second mother without cutting out the first one.

THE SEARCH

The search is a symbolic journey into the past. Everyone who had embarked upon it described it in graphic detail. They came to the interviews with their laboriously researched genealogies stuffed in boxes, folders and bags. It made me realise how much I have taken my own heritage for granted. I have no direct access to a formal family history. What I know has been absorbed here and there over the years from stories, letters, family funerals and celebrations, and photograph albums. We make links through generations without even thinking: we attribute a tendency in the males to be greedy and put on weight to an Austrian strain; my son's artistic gifts come straight from a grandmother; when my sons exhibit unpleasing characteristics I jokingly attribute these to my husband's side of the family. From my conversations with people who had searched for their birth parents, it became clear to me that the search is of vital importance, not so much as a means to an end, but as a healing psychological process in itself.

A search can take weeks, months or years; it is both an intellectual exercise and an intense emotional journey into the past. Adoptees often start searching before they are fully aware that they are doing so. Interviewees remember rifling through locked desks, boxes, or secret places to get a glimpse of their birth certificate or adoption papers when they were young. After reaching the age of eighteen they might think of searching on and off for years until something triggers them off. Once started, the search seems to gain a momentum of its own – indeed it becomes something of an obsession. The atmosphere in St Catherine's House is recalled with affection. Friendships are made along the way through the swapping of dramas, coincidences and advice. Relatives and friends are roped in to help. And at the end of the day many who have searched volunteer as contact leaders for NORCAP so they can put their experience to good use.

Research, formerly regarded as dry as dust, becomes an exciting detective puzzle as bits and pieces of personal history get discovered. There are a number of stages searchers need to go through to obtain information. Not all adoptees need to go through every stage if they already have relevant information. Others pay search agencies to do the search for them, though NORCAP recommends people to do their own research to give them time to internalise the information.

The first step for those who have no information at all is to apply for an application form for access to birth records. This can be obtained in England and Wales from the General Register Office (CA Section), Tichfield; and from the General Register Offices in Edinburgh and Belfast. If an adoption took place before 12 November, 1975, arrangements will be made locally or at St Catherine's House for the adoptee to see a counsellor before information from the birth record can be obtained. Those adopted after this date can choose whether they want to see a counsellor. Nicky Salway, who has been a birth records counsellor at St Catherine's House for ten years, sees her task as 'giving people in the short time available as much information as possible in terms of what they can do and where they can go. I never try to stop people searching because if they want to search nothing is going to stop them. But it is important to help them to do it properly.' The counsellor will provide basic information from the adoption order, including the original name, the name of the birth mother, and possibly the birth father, and the name of the court where the order was made.

After years of vociferous pressure from interested parties, Tichfield now maintains a National Contact Register, though it charges for the service. The service is not widely known about, but if an adoptee applies for a birth certificate he or she will be given the name and address of any relatives who have entered their names on the register, or an intermediary contact address. (NORCAP strongly recommends the use of a third-party address.) There is no provision however for information to be transmitted to relatives who have registered, the onus for contact remaining with the adoptee. NORCAP also keeps its own register where birth parents may place their names as an indication that they wish to be found.

The absence of a name on either register should not be taken as an indication of lack of interest. If a link has not been made then it is up to the adoptee to decide whether to take the search further by obtaining a copy of the birth certificate from St Catherine's House in London. The birth certificate contains the date and place of birth, the original name, the mother's name and occupation, the mother's address at the time, the name and address of the person who registered the birth, the date of registration and the name of the registrar. It may also include the father's name and occupation.

Many adopted people feel that this information satisfies their needs. Those who want to go on and trace their parents can get additional information from a variety of sources. They can write to the original adoption society, or the appropriate local authority. If the name of the society or local authority is not known, the counsellor will provide the authorisation to ask the court for this information. Scottish law gives an adopted person direct access to the court process papers. If the adoption society no longer exists, the British Agencies for Adoption and Fostering (BAAF) will probably be able to indicate where the records are now held. These records should contain detailed information about the circumstances in which the adoption was made and may include a letter from the birth mother.

As the adoptee is trying to pick up a trail at least eighteen and possibly forty or fifty years old, the birth mother is unlikely to be found still living at the original address. It is at this point that the search can become a sleuthing exercise. Possible avenues of research can be the marriage and birth registers at St Catherine's House. It is from these that adoptees often find out that they have siblings. Electoral registers and telephone directories also come in handy. Door-to-door enquiries in the street or village of the original address can sometimes yield information.

In any event, the technicalities, the financial cost, and the time spent can be extremely daunting. It is therefore well worth becoming a member of NORCAP, which is a national organisation with members in most parts of the country who can check records and registers in their localities. It also organises search days in St Catherine's House. More importantly NORCAP will put the searcher in touch with a contact who will be on hand to advise, encourage and support members through what is inevitably an emotionally charged and frustrating experience. This contact can also act as an intermediary between the adoptee and members of the birth family if a reunion is sought.

It is very difficult for birth parents to search unless they know their child's adopted name because they do not have access to identifying information and agencies do not readily co-operate. If they know the birthday of their child, and the date of the adoption order there is one hit-and-miss way of unearthing information in St Catherine's House. They can search in the index of the Adopted Children register and order adoption certificates for likely candidates around the adoption date in the hope that one might tally with the birth date. It can be an expensive, time-consuming and ultimately unsuccessful exercise. On one level the search is about data locked away in indices; on another it is more like John Bunyan's *Pilgrim's Progress*. Before he reaches his destination on his symbolic journey, Christian has to travel through the Slough of Despond, the Interpreter's

House, the House Beautiful, the Valley of Humiliation, the Valley of the Shadow of Death, Vanity Fair, Doubting Castle, and the Delectable Mountains. These are places which will sound familiar to most searchers. Some will falter or fall by the wayside, but if they persevere they will feel they have achieved something of great personal significance. This was certainly the case for James, aged thirty-seven, who gave me a beautiful account of a classic search.

'I must say that I consider my adoptive parents my real parents because they were the only ones I ever knew and grew up with and loved, and so for me they are my real parents. I was ignorant of 1975 but if I had known I wouldn't have been interested. I knew my mother had been a single parent and had been in difficult circumstances without support of family and had had to place me for adoption. I knew my natural father was an American serviceman who had gone back to the USA so was unreachable in my eyes. Anything outside a twenty-mile radius was outside my ken.

'One thing that may have made a small impact on me was that I had two birth certificates – a long one which said I was adopted, and a short one. So I was aware that there was something slightly different about my situation. On one occasion when I was a teenager I was looking through the cashbox and came across an envelope marked "James's Papers" and I knew there was information about my natural parents. I looked at it and saw the name I had had before the adoption.

That was all I took in. It felt strange for a moment and then I put it back in the box and forgot about it.

'My father died after I finished my under-graduate course. I considered tracing maybe a couple of times. I suppose I had a heightened awareness that there might be someone out there who was wondering what had happened to me and I was interested in knowing what had happened to her. It was information I wanted. I wasn't looking for anything to complete an emotional part of me. I made a conscious decision not to do any tracing until my mother had passed on because I didn't want to risk spoiling what we had – a totally loving, normal relationship. Her death opened the way to searching without fear of the consequences. Also, "James's Papers" in the box were now mine to do what I liked with. My wife and I had had a baby and I went through the experience of being a parent and knew what it was to see a child born and to have created a life. That was the strongest impulse of all, that maybe someone had felt that towards me once, and that perhaps through no fault of her own she had to give me up for adoption.

'The box contained a letter from the adoption society to my parents and the court order with my natural mother's name and mine on it. I looked upon them and began thinking of my natural mother as a person with an identity – which was the first time I thought of her as a woman with physical form. I paid a visit to my local Social Services and said I wanted to trace and was told I *had to have counselling which turned out to be very good. The social worker understood my motivations and asked questions to satisfy herself that my approach was right. The advice she gave me was exactly the level I wanted to help me understand why I was doing this and the possible outcome. She pointed out that the person I found might not be a person I liked, or might not like me; that I might be rejected or that I might end up embroiled in a difficult family situation. I decided very early on that if I didn't search I would regret it, and if I did search I might regret it, so the better option was to search.*

'When my birth certificate arrived I got a buzz that I was embarking on an adventure – a bit of detective work with a lot of human interest. I opened it up and read my name and my mother's full name and address. That was the first step. Then a note of disappointment crept in because my father's name was just a line. That highlighted that something was incomplete. Up to this point I had never considered my life before Mum and Dad. My roots were with my adoptive parents and I viewed their tree and ancestors as mine. Now I was being forced to consider that I did have an existence before that time. And I felt a sense of betrayal, a feeling that I was just breaking loose a little bit. That feeling of guilt didn't last too long and I rationalised it with the thought that just because you're looking for something else doesn't mean you're taking away from what you've had.

'The adoption society was very helpful and

showed me my file. They had made good records at the time and, thank goodness, had kept them. They gave me my certificate of baptism with the names of godparents which was nice. I also learnt about my brother – my older brother. That was a shock. I was stunned for a day. The thought that I wasn't alone, that there was another one like me. I'm certain that my parents didn't know; they would surely have told me. When I learnt about my brother it took me back to when I was nineteen and went to the doctor over a minor ailment. The doctor looked through my records and asked, "Have you forgiven your brother for making you drink shampoo?" and I said, "Sorry, I haven't got a brother." And he said, "Yes you have, it's in your record." And I said, "Sorry, you've got the wrong record." I walked out thinking there had been a foul-up in the records. Then all these years later I realised he had been right. [James had been able to trace his brother quite easily because he learnt the name of his adoptive parents from the adoption society, and after exchanging letters they met.]

'I then went on tracing my natural mother. I felt I had to visit the address on my birth certificate and the church where I was christened. It was a lovely church and a lovely sunny day. I like churches and there was a tremendous feeling of warmth with the light coming through the windows – and the choir was practising and the hymns were beautiful. I put my name in the visitors' book. That was a moment of great emotion for me to

imagine that I had been there as a baby with my natural mother and godparents. I found somebody involved in the church and told her my story and she said she would make some discreet enquiries, particularly about my godparents. I went to visit the doctor who had been the student doctor and was now the senior practitioner. All these leads came to a dead-end but it was interesting and built up a picture.

'From another source I found out the name of my godmother and went to see her. It turned out that she had been with my mother in a hostel and had not known her long. She had gone into hospital to have a baby and when she came out my mother and us two boys had left with no forwarding address, but she remembered that she had been totally devoted to us and had been desperately trying to keep us well, and so it confirmed the good picture I was building up of her.

'I found out about NORCAP, which I joined, and got the booklet about tracing. Then it was off to St Catherine's House and records and electoral rolls. I spent half a day on the death registers because I knew she had been ill. Happily she wasn't there. I found her birth certificate and decided to learn about her family. So I did some electoral roll searching and found information on my natural grandmother and aunties right to the turn of the century. On another visit I started on marriages and found hers. Then I went to births and found two families which could have been hers. When I got home I went to the local library and got to the

telephone directories and found the entry of her husband's name. So now I had her name, address and telephone number. So I went to my social worker with all the details and asked her to act as intermediary. From having started out mildly interested, I had ended up being fascinated by the detective work.

'I had built up a mental picture of my mother, but when I located her I became obsessed by what she would think of me, what she would say, and what her situation was. Shortly afterwards the social worker called me to discuss her reply. She had written a very nice letter to the social worker saying, "Yes, I'm the right person. This is a little bit about me. I don't know what he'll think of me, having to give him up. I'm worried he'll think badly of me." There was a little note to myself saying, "Hello, I was your mum for a year," and bits of information.

'She had always been open with her husband. One of the daughters had died of something which immediately put us in a flat spin. Our daughter was thin and a bit unwell so we were worried that she might have the same thing. We had our daughter tested and it was OK. I had an invitation to write, so I wrote her my life history and she wrote back her life history. And I took to her immediately. We exchanged more letters, being honest and intimate with our feelings for each other.

'One Saturday when I was cleaning the car there was a telephone call and my wife said, "It's your *mother." I am still sensitive about the terminology. She said it in a nice way but it hurt. I call my natural mother by her first name. In the early days I would studiously call her my natural mother but between my wife and myself it's slipped a bit, and I say Mother while my adoptive mother is still always Mum. My mum's death made a tremendous impact on me, it really did. I miss her and think about her a lot and that strength of association with her makes it difficult sometimes to relate to my natural mother. I'm more distant towards her than I should be because of this great sense of loyalty to my mum. I've written telling her this so I think she understands. We had a nice chat on the telephone and arranged to meet.'*

James and his brother had a reunion with his mother and her family. Since then the relationship has settled down comfortably. They have met several times and correspond regularly. His brother leads a somewhat chaotic and fraught life, but James was warned of this by the social worker and does not involve himself or feel responsible. Having found his mother he felt that it was important to go on and find his father. His mother gave him the few details she remembered and he undertook a long-distance search with what amounted to military precision, even to the extent of keeping a detailed log. He became a member of TRACE (Transatlantic Children's Enterprise) who provided him with military addresses. He also used a search consultant in California and finally got in touch with some genealogical groups in the state where he thought his father lived.

It was an amateur historian who finally tracked him down and acted as intermediary. They have corresponded and James has arranged to visit him and his family. He just wants to offer the hand of friendship and learn a bit about him and his antecedents.

James had his share of good luck, but his search turned out so well largely because he took wise precautions and paced himself sensibly. He was fortunate in having a sympathetic and helpful social worker but he made good use of her advice and services as an intermediary. A lot of grief can be avoided by using intermediaries; they are very careful when they make the first contact, usually writing a neutral letter which would be understood by the recipient but not by any casual reader. They might, for instance, pretend to be doing family research for a client whom they identify by the original name, suggesting the recipient make contact if further information is wanted.

James saved time by the sensible use of records in St Catherine's House but he took time to absorb material and make judgements about what to do next. He was careful to correspond with his brother, mother and father before embarking on meetings. This way they too had time to learn about him and his motives for searching and to make their own decisions about whether to meet him or not. He could have stopped at any point if the picture he was building up had made him uneasy. It is clear from his account that his search gave him a great deal of interest, comfort and pleasure. It enabled him to add his original genealogical history to his own adoptive history without one detracting from the other.

REUNIONS

While searching can remain an individual pursuit, reunions involve the making of brand-new relationships within a highly emotional context. All of us continuously create new relationships as we grow up. First we learn to relate to the members of our immediate family, then to friends outside the home and teachers at school. Later we build up relationships with partners. In marriage families of two origins are brought together, and in step-families there is an even more complex network of relationships. All additional relationships need working out but we are helped to manage them by acquired experience, accumulated knowledge, custom and example.

Members in the adoption triangle who reunite are forging new relationships in comparatively uncharted territory. There is very little in the way of research or information to help them. Not much seems to have been written about the impact and consequences of reunions on the participants. There are no books on reunion etiquette or advice on the bookshelves. Elders in the family cannot pose as role models. The relationships have to be worked out largely by instinct and common sense.

The word reunion is perhaps misleading. When members of birth families make contact they are not reuniting but meeting for the first time – except, of course, in the case of mother and child. Yet it is a reunion because a lost member is being re-introduced into the family. They are strangers yet they have genetic characteristics in common. They have different life histories yet share the same heritage. They have not bonded over the years yet are loaded down by emotions from the past and hopes for the future.

Very few of the people I interviewed told me of bad reunion experiences. I might have been surprised by this if I had not already spoken to Pam Hodgkins about her survey. She found that over eighty per cent of those who had met members of their birth families considered that they had been welcomed and accepted, and spoke of their relationships in positive terms. Most of the partners and family members had been supportive. Her conclusion was that 'lasting satisfactory relationships do develop between adult adoptees and found members of their birth family.'

Good outcomes to these reunions depend on so many personal characteristics – like matching expectations, goodwill, patience, and sensitivity – that it is difficult to sketch out a perfect blueprint. But from the following stories it is possible to generalise about some of the factors that make for good reunions and some of those that contribute to bad ones. The first was recounted to me by Wendy, aged forty-three, and her daughter Irene, aged twenty-six, who asked to be interviewed together.

They were shy to start with but obviously delighted in each other's company.

Wendy: *I had Irene through a chap I didn't really know. I met him at a dance and one night he brought me home and forced me up against a brick wall and that's how I had Irene. I was fifteen and my parents found out when I was four months pregnant. I sort of knew; I had been writing to magazines saying I had these funny symptoms, and my mother found one of the letters and went absolutely mad. It was shame for the family and everything was taken out of my hands. I was sent to a Mother and Baby home and wasn't allowed to be seen in the streets.*

All the way through I wasn't going to be able to keep Irene. The birth was OK. Irene was so pretty and I nursed her for six weeks. You had the baby but you knew in the back of your mind that she had to go. It really, really was a wrench. The first few months were dreadful. I went home and had to pretend nothing had happened. I used to cry for years afterwards. I used to write to the Adoption Society asking how she was. Luckily Irene has one letter I wrote, saying I really did love her and didn't want to give her up and hopefully she would have a better home and a life than she would have had with me. I always hoped that I had done the right thing, that she would have a nice home with a nice family, but it was never mentioned again in my family. I got on with my life, got married and had two girls, but I always thought of her and wondered how she was growing up. When she was eighteen I wondered whether she would get in contact. I did think that one day we would meet.

Irene: *I was told quite a few times when I was very young that I had been adopted but I didn't understand it because I thought my mother was coming back. At the age of eight it suddenly clicked that my mother wasn't going to come and fetch me. There was a tin of papers and I used to look in it; I liked seeing my original name. I was very different from my family. We argued a lot and I just didn't fit in. I didn't want to be like them. In adolescence the arguing got much worse. I couldn't do anything right. I had an older brother who was their natural child. He and I fought all the time because he wasn't very bright and I was cleverer, which caused problems. When I was seventeen they decided to move into a two-bedroomed house with my brother. So that was it and I moved out into a bedsit.*

I got my birth certificate when I was nineteen but the search took five years on and off. I did it all by myself. It was a nice secret — it was mine. I was looking to meet her and was sure I would. Everyone cautioned me, especially the counsellor, but I thought, 'My case will be different.' When I found her I got a friend to phone up.

Wendy: *I had just arrived back from work with two carrier bags of shopping and my daughter was playing in the kitchen when the phone went. This voice asked whether I had had Irene in 1963. There was a ringing in my head which said, 'Yes, yes, yes.' I remember asking whether the adoptive parents knew because I didn't want to hurt them. I couldn't say much because of my daughter being there. It was a shock, yet such a happy feeling. I took a deep breath and sat down. I wanted to scream and shout, 'She's found me, she's found me,' but I couldn't say anything to anybody. I thought about it the whole weekend. I had told my husband before we were married but there again we had never spoken about it. I rang back the friend and asked for Irene to write to me. Two weeks went by and I still hadn't said anything, by which time I was beginning to feel really ill. My husband asked if I was all right because I was going grey; a heavy weight was keeping me down. In the end I burst out crying and told him what had happened. He said, 'It's wonderful, you must meet her.' Then I had the trouble of having to tell the girls, because you bring them up to have certain standards. I had believed for so many years that I had done something terrible, something shameful. When I told my youngest daughter she thought it was wonderful. The oldest one thought it was a joke at first, but when I convinced her she said, 'Oh! I like having an older sister.' I couldn't believe the reaction. If anyone knew what I went through and how I would lead up to telling them. Everybody was wonderful. My friends are dying to meet her. People are surprising – how accepting they are. For me it's such a happy relief not having to carry that terrible thing around with me any more.*

The family's together and I haven't got a child out there any more – and everybody knows. It's all out in the open. We wrote long letters to each other and when my husband read hers he said, 'You are so alike.' We arranged to meet in a restaurant in London. I just cried when I saw her. We stayed together for hours and hours. It was as if we had known each other for ages; not like strangers meeting.

Irene: *The meeting just seemed like the final step. When I told my adoptive parents that I had traced my mother they said they didn't want any more contact, so I said, 'That's it.' I hadn't had had much contact anyway and should have said it years ago. I feel sad about the years I've missed but I'm so glad with what we have and I'm not angry with anyone. It's like life starting again. For the first time in my life I feel secure and accepted for what I am. I feel I've got my own family on my own side now, when it was always my husband's family.*

Wendy: *I was angry that they already had a son which I hadn't known. I had put so much trust in that family, that they were going to do the right thing and bring her up with lots of love – all the things I couldn't do. When Irene met me she found out that all the information she had been given by the Social Services who had done the adoption placement was a complete fabrication. I think you have to tell the truth, otherwise one lie leads to another. She's been brilliant about the rape though I'm still angry about it – with society in general and my parents, I think.*

The crux of this story seems to me to be acceptance – an important ingredient for a successful reunion. Wendy found that when she came out in the open the people around her accepted her past and her child – not grudgingly but with joy. It proved so much easier to tell her children than she had imagined. Irene accepted the circumstances of her conception. Wendy is trying to accept the fact that the adoption had not been the happy one she had built her hopes on. They were able to discuss these things without blaming each other. The adoptive parents were not able to accept the reunion but the relationship had obviously broken down earlier.

Sometimes people who trace find their birth mothers in less well-off circumstances than themselves. This can be a tricky situation to handle and requires a great deal of tact and sensitivity. Barbara, aged forty-five, had been adopted by a professional couple who had plenty of money. She embarked on a search after both her adoptive parents had died and found her mother and two half-sisters.

'I wanted a relationship with my birth mother and never got it. Every important person in my life aside from my husband and children had died. My mother was sixty-eight and basically said, "Accept me for what I am and give us time." But I hadn't known her for forty years and was impatient. She lived in a council house and was on supplementary benefit. Her husband was ill upstairs. She was a hoarder and kept everybody's rubbish. I helped her to refurbish her house and I bought her a washing

machine because I was so disgusted that she had to do the washing by hand. One day I was helping to decorate her bathroom and we talked and I gave her my view that her family didn't pull their weight. They would get together in an emergency but weren't close like I was with my daughters. My mother seemed odd. I knew something was wrong but couldn't put my finger on it. Two days later I got a letter from my sister saying how dare I say that the family wasn't close after they had welcomed me with open arms. I went to see my mother and tried to have it out with her but she didn't want to know about the letter. She said it was between me and my sister but I know she had instigated it. I just wanted to help her like any human being.'

It is understandable that Barbara wanted to help her mother who was poorer than she was, but she went about it in a clumsy way. She only succeeded in undermining her sisters and forcing her mother to take sides. Cindy, who is the same age, managed a similar situation very differently.

'Before I met my mother letters and photos went backwards and forwards. When I got the first photo I couldn't believe it wasn't me and apparently she had the same reaction. By this time I had clicked that she must be married to my father but we didn't talk about this in the letters. We corresponded for about five months before arranging to meet in a hotel. I drove up alone because I didn't

think it was right even to take my husband. I
brought champagne and flowers and put on six
different lots of clothes and make-up. A knock
came on the door. I opened it and said, "Hello,
Mum." It just came naturally. We gave ourselves
a big cuddle and didn't cry. It was emotional and
a bit tense. She arrived at 1.00 p.m. and we talked
until 10.00 p.m. I said, "You're married to my
father." And she said, "You monkey, I wanted to
tell you." It was wonderful news. She had had no
alternative when I was born. She was on her own
because my father, who was in the army, was married with two children. When he came out of the
army he got divorced; they married and had two
more girls. So I learnt that I had two full sisters
who knew nothing about me yet. My mother often
says what a shame it is that we have missed so
many years, but I say it doesn't matter because
we've got lots of time ahead of us.

'Mum and my sisters came here for a week with
all their children. We had a fantastic week doing
everything, and it was one big laugh from beginning to end. I feel that I've never been out of the
family. Every birthday my parents had remembered me. My mum thought she had given her baby
away for good and didn't think she would ever
find me. She tells me it's a miracle. It's given me
such pleasure giving them things. I feel I have to
make up for all the Christmases I've missed. But I
go very carefully and always consult my sisters
first. I've given them a washing machine and a
phone upstairs and a smoke alarm. I don't believe

*my sisters are resentful. We are planning to move
to the country and have them live with us, which
my sisters think is a great idea.*

'*I hadn't had a particularly happy situation with
my adoptive parents. I don't know whether it was
the chemical mix, or whether I felt unwanted, but
we are so different in thought, outlook on life and
attitudes. I told them I was going to search, and
they understood and were pleased when I did find
my mother and wanted to meet her. At the meeting
my adoptive mother said, "Thank you for allowing
us to have her." And my mother said, "Thank you
for looking after her for all these years." I have
tried to reassure them and have made sure not to
hurt them. We have a much better relationship
now. I feel complete and peaceful and much hap-
pier inside. Everybody says I've changed. I don't
believe anyone has lost anything in this whole
thing. We've all gained something.*'

I have heard of cases where adoptees have felt upset
and bitter at finding their parents had married. Perhaps
in the last resort this is a matter of temperament. For
Cindy it was a joyful outcome and she felt no resentment. It is certainly very helpful for a birth mother to
have a partner who is as anxious as she is to reunite
with the lost child.

Cindy's description of the first meeting is very typical.
Reunions are generally arranged on neutral ground. The
sense of anticipation is agony. What will she be like?
Will I like her? Will she like me? How shall I greet
her? In the event, most interviewees reported initial

conversations that went on for hours and hours while life stories were swapped and explanations given. At these first meetings one of the strongest emotions is the sense of wonderment, of touching flesh, and comparing genetic features. Then follows a honeymoon period when the novelty and excitement is still keeping everyone on a high while introductions are made with other family members. The next stage is the crucial one when curiosity has been satisfied and all the parties have to get down to sorting out the amount of contact and the new roles in the family. This is the time when it is wise to be cautious.

Tania, aged thirty-nine, felt that problems arose for her because she hadn't given enough consideration to what she wanted from her reunion. She had had a very happy adoptive home. Her father was dead and her mother senile when she did her search.

'I have no regrets about the way I approached my birth mother. I used an intermediary and gave her the chance and time to think about whether she wanted to meet me. But what I never gave a single thought to was what would happen after the meeting. On the train going to see her all I could think about was whether she would be a mirror-image of me, and would I like her. It's a ludicrous thing to admit but I wondered whether she would have a Liverpudlian accent. Did the fact that she had been through three marriages mean that she was a loose women? Would I like my half-sister? Why had she given me away when maybe she had married my father? I was very twitchy and nervous.

She wasn't a mirror-image of me (apparently I'm just like my father) but I knew immediately who she was at the station from the look of sheer terror on her face. I didn't know what to call her until she suggested that I call her by her Christian name. I couldn't see her as my mother at all.

'*We went to have lunch at a hotel and she said, "Right, I'll tell you the whole story," and out it all came. She had tried to abort me but had really cared about my father, who was not one of her husbands, and had regretted not marrying him. She was obviously very disturbed by the way I looked so like him. I was hugely amused that I might have gone down the lavatory. I stayed five days with her and was nicely surprised. Her husband had always known about me and was perfectly relaxed. I like my mother – she is a nice person. There is a social difference between us but she's well read and has done a lot for herself.*

'*It all began to get out of hand when my half-sister got in touch with me. She's a ferocious woman, very direct, like a bull in a china shop. I felt overwhelmed by her. She wanted me to visit her so that she could show me off to all her friends in the office. The crunch came at Christmas when my sister phoned up and said, "Are you going home for Christmas?" I was totally astonished. She had referred to her home as my home and I said, "No, as a matter of fact I shall be visiting my mother in the nursing home." Then my mum died and I met Tony and got engaged. This was a time of high emotion for me and in the middle of it all my birth mother's husband died. She expected me to go over for the funeral as her daughter and offer a shoulder to weep on. But I had my own hassles and didn't think I needed to go. When Tony and I got married we decided to invite my mother and sister to the wedding but as guests, not relatives. They were not in the front pew. Some months later I got this dreadful letter from my sister. It all came out then – how hurt they were about Christmas, the funeral and the wedding. She was very angry and said I had been upsetting my mother. I wrote back saying that my relationship with my mother was my own business, not hers. I didn't know what the hell to do about it all.*

'Eventually I asked my mother to come and talk about it. I met her for the first time on my home ground and felt a bit safer. I put all my cards on the table which I should have done right from the start. I told her that I had always wanted to find her and was very pleased I had. I liked her very much, but because we were strangers I couldn't just push a light switch and start loving her. I didn't want her to fulfil the role of mother, or me the role of child. I wanted to remain friends from a distance. She was very good about it and seemed to understand how I felt. She lay low for a while and we exchanged cards and phone calls.'

Trying to match expectations is the most delicate aspect of reunions. Some people are looking for a parent–child relationship in a spirit of repossession. Others want the sort of contact one might have with a special aunt or godparent. For many, a distant contact is enough. It may be difficult to know in advance what sort of contact is appropriate, but it is helpful to try and be as clear as possible because difficulties do arise if expectations are in conflict. In Cindy's case everyone wanted the same thing. Her parents were married and wanted their child back in the family. Cindy felt she had found her 'real' parents though this did not mean she abandoned her adoptive ones. Tania wasn't looking for a substitute mother. She was still grieving for her adoptive mother who had died in the middle of it all. And she is probably still angry with her birth mother. I suspect that she found the story of the attempted abortion distressing rather than amusing. Family gatherings like weddings and christenings often highlight this vexed question of status. Step-families have to wrestle with exactly the same problems. They can be worked out if people do not presume they have a right to certain roles, if they do not take offence if these roles are not assigned to them. It is also worth remembering that relationships don't need to be set in concrete from the beginning. They can evolve and change over the years as people get to know each other and grow more trustful.

REUNIONS INVOLVE OTHERS

What people most fear about reunions is being rejected. This fear often puts people off searching altogether. This possibility is usually stressed by birth record counsellors, though outright rejection is the exception rather than the norm. Intermediaries in reunions have told me that even if birth mothers react negatively to the initial contact, given time and a sensitive approach they usually come round in the end. Ariel Bruce, who runs a private search agency, put it like this: 'I would honestly say that we can turn round eighteen out of twenty initial rejections given the right approach. Absolute refusals usually come by return of post. I might then telephone and tentatively find out what this is about. If a birth mother is worried about the adoptive parents I point out that the adoptee is an adult. If I can assure them that my client has no intention of making outrageous demands, or turning up on the doorstep, the door usually opens.'

A person who turns up unannounced on the doorstep is likely to be turned away because the person who is found has not had time to prepare for such an encounter. People can't think straight when they are in a state of shock. The doorstep approach doesn't happen very often but I was told a sad story by a woman who did this against her better judgement. It was almost as if she couldn't stop herself. She drove to the village where she knew her mother lived and sought her out at her place of work. Her mother spoke to her kindly but gave her no explanations and asked her to make no further contact.

The way the approach is made can be crucial, but there are often more complex reasons why relationships do not get off the ground or disintegrate after the initial contact. The following story is told by Kay, an attractive, highly articulate woman aged twenty-three, whose adoptive parents divorced when she was sixteen.

'I saw a social worker who asked me why I wanted to search. I didn't know – I just had to do it. At first I fooled myself that it was just curiosity and if I got a photo, that would be enough. But it's not and I don't think it ever can be. I think if you start you are looking for a relationship. My social worker spent a lot of time preparing me for the fact that my birth mother might not want to meet me, that she had a life of her own. This idea of being unwanted has always surrounded me, so in the forefront of my mind was the thought that my mother might not want to know. On the other hand I sort of sympathised and thought she might have been through a bad time and would be curious and want to see me.

'In the event I found my father first, almost

by coincidence. I keep hearing of coincidences in searches. I was in the library studying for an exam, got bored and started looking for his name in the telephone directories. I didn't know what town he lived in, but the first book I pulled down was London and his name and initials were there. I rang up and a woman answered and said he was out, so I said I'd ring later. I was nervous and not sure I had got the right person. I hadn't really thought of him as such, not the way I had thought about my mother. But I rang back and he answered the phone and I asked him if he minded being asked a couple of questions. When he had answered them I said, "Well, I think I'm your daughter", and he said, "Yes, very probably." Later he said that as soon as his wife told him that a girl had called, a bit mysterious, he had been sure his time was up.

'*He asked me what I wanted to do and I said my ultimate goal was to meet him. He asked me to write and explain everything. I was curious to know the circumstances of his affair with my mother and wrote asking if it had been a long-term affair, a short-term affair or a one-night stand. He sent me a strange letter which I subsequently destroyed in a fit of anger, saying that I was not the result of a one-night stand but everything in life is relative.*

'*We met in London at the station. I knew what he looked like from his written description. He never sent a photo, though I had asked for one. During a five-hour lunch we talked about various issues including what sort of music we liked. He kept saying how curious that we had so much in common. Later we went for a walk in the park and he came back to the affair with my mother. He told me all about it, where he had taken her on weekends, that he had been terribly attracted to her. He said what a relief it was to be talking like this. He had never told anyone. He had been engaged to his wife when he had the affair with my mother so she knew what had gone on but they had never talked about it. It was as if I was his confessor for a day.*

'He and his wife hadn't had any children. I asked him if he'd told her that he was meeting me. He said he hadn't meant to but as he was getting ready to go out he had told her the truth and walked out before they could discuss it. When we said good-bye, on impulse I kissed him on the cheek. I thought it was a gesture one should make towards one's father. Two days later I got a letter in which he said he'd been very touched by my saying good-bye like that and that he had hopes of more meetings. There seemed to be a lot of hope in that letter for a relationship. But then he didn't reply to my letters, so I wrote asking whether he intended to reply or not. He wrote saying he had reconsidered. He hardly ever thought about me and thought it better that we discontinue contact. It's occurred to me, and it's something I've learnt from NORCAP, that one shouldn't be impulsive. I was impulsive. I wanted him to meet me and didn't give him time to think about it. He said in his letter that he'd

met me after a brief moment of weakness and curiosity and if he'd had time to come to his senses he wouldn't have agreed to meet me in the first place.'

It may be that Kay's father is not a free agent. It sounds as if his wife may be against a continuing relationship. Not having had a child of her own she may feel threatened by the appearance of the child who must have caused her pain in the early days. The point to be made here is that reunions do not just depend on the main participants but on others in the family system as well, and they can easily go wrong if spouses or siblings cannot handle the situation. Another reason for his rejection may be that Kay reminds him of her mother and an affair that was obviously important to him. Kay picked herself up and went on searching for her mother with renewed vigour. She was studying in Paris when her mother was located. With remarkable honesty Kay explained why this relationship foundered.

'When she phoned me up I was stunned. It was very difficult to take it all in. I dread to think of her phone bill. We talked for two hours about all sorts of things. It was euphoria – we'd found each other at last. She told me she was married and that I had a half-brother and sister. Her husband had always known about me. She told me she was coming to visit me. Our first meeting was at the airport and it was wonderful. I identified with her at once. She is my height, my weight, my shoe-size – everything. We were very close from the moment

she got off the plane. She stayed for a week and it was very intense. One doesn't know how to describe these things but the best way is to say we had a physical lesbian affair. I'm not a lesbian, and have never had an affair with a woman before or after. I wanted physical contact but it was definitely she who made the first move from anything that was just ordinary affection and I didn't put up any resistance. It continued for the week and it was fine but I realise she felt guilty about it and I didn't know how to cope with that. I don't think I ever felt it was wrong. She made me feel very much wanted. She told me she had found it difficult to relate physically to her other children because she was always thinking of me. It made me feel special.

'We talked about a lot of things but at the end we started to have arguments about very fundamental things. I said things without realising that sort of condemned her relationship with my father, like one should be careful if you go to bed with a man. She was shocked that my parents had got divorced. It probably made her feel guilty, and to be absolutely honest it is something I blame her for. She was the one who sent me to my adoptive parents. She had chosen parents with plenty of money and the fact that the picture turned out differently made her defensive. She started to say that she thought she had done the right thing by me then, and still does.

'When she returned home she rang every day, and we wrote letters daily. Sometimes I thought,

"I'm in very deep and don't know how to get out."
She wanted me to go home, meaning her house
and meet her husband and children. She had
decided not to say anything to her husband but it
came out that she told him I had initiated the affair
against her will. She made me promise not to tell
anybody either which I tried not to do because I
didn't think it was a promise I could keep. I told
my boyfriend at the time. He was extremely understanding and I don't know what I would have done
without him. Not that I thought it was wrong, but
I thought it was odd. And I still can't explain it.
He said it was like bridging a gap. If you have a
child, it is an intimate relationship between baby
and mother. I wonder if it's something that stems
from our relationship, or something she had been
doing before. I can't say.

'I went back to my social worker because I was
really confused about it, and it really hit me
because she said she was going to put me in touch
with people involved in incest. I hadn't thought of
it as incest. I think I went along with the physical
contact because I so wanted to please her and I
thought being my mother she would know what
was best. My mother said I reminded her of my
father and I thought, "She's reliving her affair with
him through me." In hindsight I've been offended
by this. What also offends me is that in our rows
she brings back all the hurt she had with my father
and tells me that I'm stubborn and hurtful like
him. On the one hand she wanted to relive the

good times, and on the other I get blamed for the nasty side of things.

'The intense relationship had the seeds of doom in it. We couldn't discuss it. We had a terrible row and fell out completely. The only contact I have with my mother now is through my sister. I feel I'm allowed to write to her because my mother's interested in knowing where I am. I think the only way we can stay in contact is at a distance. I want friendship and equality, but she wants a mother—daughter relationship. I get this feeling that we'll never get on as two adults until I get married and have children of my own. In spite of everything I'm glad I searched. I know who I am and I see that as very positive. It is better to know than not to know. It would be easy to start thinking that both my parents have rejected me twice, but that is too simplistic. It is not like that.'

Genetic sexual attraction is a phenomenon that is beginning to be better understood as it becomes more widely revealed. Without the benefit of any special knowledge Kay gave some understandable reasons why the physical contact with her mother became sexually intimate. They felt an immediate sense of physical identity in an emotionally charged atmosphere. There was a gap to be bridged with none of the formal social restraints against incest that get built into normal evolving relationships between parents and children. Both mother and daughter were desperate for affection, and wanted so much to be pleased and to please each other.

The Post-Adoption Centre and NORCAP have been

dealing with an increasing number of cases of incest in reunions in the last few years as people become less reluctant to seek help. A worker at PAC told me that the cases involve mothers and sons; mothers and daughters; siblings; and occasionally fathers and daughters. 'We find that what is common across all ages and combinations of people who reunite is a feeling of obsession and being in love – with all the accompanying signs like longing for telephone calls; partners feeling left out; huge energy being invested in the relationship. But in a minority of cases fully-blown affairs do develop and can have dire consequences.'

The worker went on to tell me the little that is known about incestuous reunions. 'We know how much feeling and yearning gets generated in reunions. Deep emotions are touched and some adults find that the only vehicle they know for expressing these is through sexual contact. It is a sort of claiming process, yet there are no organised rituals around it, as there are around marriage, for instance.

'Sometimes sexual attraction occurs between people who resemble each other strongly. There seems to be a great need to touch, feel and make physical contact. Mothers claim babies through smell and touch and by exploring all the nooks and crannies. These feelings can get re-aroused as they try to reclaim the lost years. There can be hidden agendas as well. A son's anger might find expression in a need to have sexual domination over his mother. A mother might feel too bad about herself and guilty to be able to refuse. Inappropriate passion can be fuelled by all sorts of hidden emotions, fantasies and projections.'

It is certainly clear from Kay's story that everyone was wrestling with unresolved emotional problems. Kay was angry and blamed her mother for her unhappy adoptive life. Kay's mother felt guilty about the adoption and was sensitive to criticism. Twenty-three years later, neither her mother nor father appeared to have got over the affair. All these underlying feelings would have contributed to the passionate start of the reunion.

I debated whether to include Kay's interview in my book and decided that while it was important not to exaggerate the phenomenon, it was important to make readers aware of the possibility arising, so that warning signs can be heeded and sensible precautions taken. Incest is after all a criminal offence, and can lead to unnecessary emotional and practical complications.

It makes sense to confine the first reunion meeting to a public location, and to a matter of hours rather than days. If people are aware of feeling sexually attracted to each other after the first meeting, they can make sure that partners or relatives are involved in further meetings. Sometimes the physical feelings can be channelled into harmless shared activities or sports. If the feelings cannot be sublimated or controlled, then it really is sensible to seek help. Talking and bringing it out in the open is useful. Because incest is associated with shame, guilt and fear, people are reluctant to talk about it, so the relationships often break up completely in recrimination and bitterness. Professional advice can help those involved to extricate themselves from tangled relationships while finding a more appropriate way to be close.

REUNIONS FROM OTHER PERSPECTIVES

Although most reunions are initiated by adoptees, sometimes adoptive parents arrange meetings to help their children, or to help them understand their children better. Chrissie and her husband did this before their adopted daughter was eighteen.

'After the birth of our son we went through five ghastly years of not having more children, not through miscarriages – just not having them. To have the apparatus and nursery all ready for a family and to have one solitary figure is just as painful as not having any children at all. We have a spinster aunt who is the focal point of the family and through her we heard that Rose, the daughter of a distant cousin, was about to go into a home. We felt we had something to offer and it was wonderful for us. We could help and get help ourselves. It appeared that her mother was as delighted as we were. It was easy to talk to Rose about her adoption because we knew the situation. We were able to tell her that in an ideal world her mother

wouldn't have wanted to give her up but as she was in such an unhappy situation she wanted something better for her. We used to send her mother the odd photo and her grandmother took a great interest, and we kept that going.

'It was always difficult to know what was going on in Rose's mind but inevitably as she grew up she felt everything in life that was difficult would have been perfect if she had been our real child. When she was fourteen I sensed that in her mind she was creating a fairytale mother who was perfect in every way that I wasn't, so I thought it would be a good idea if we all met. I had no fears about it. I'm not a jealous person and had no envy in me. I was worried that Rose might interpret our not minding as not caring. She might have said that we didn't love her as much as her brother. She's never said it but she might have thought it. She's talented at so many things but we've never managed to get her to pursue any of her talents. The minute she thinks she is getting anywhere she cuts it off. It hasn't been made easier by her brother's success. She's expecting to be a failure all the time. It is as if she is always testing us to see the limits of our commitment.

'We had a fascinating meeting, with the aunt in the middle. There was our family, and Rose's mother brought her new husband. She has never had any more children. We saw such a strong likeness between Rose and her mother. Then there was a gap and Rose didn't talk about seeing her mother again but recently she took the initiative and went *to see her by herself. She told me beforehand and I thought it was wonderful. They talked about the past which can't have been a bad thing. She's much more settled now and seems more happy and positive in herself.'*

It was easy for Chrissie to set up a meeting because the birth mother was known to her, but I also spoke to a mother who had adopted a baby boy in the traditional way and undertook the search herself. She actually met the birth mother before her son did. She felt that she had a greater understanding of her son after the meeting.

With the change in the social climate more birth parents, especially mothers, are searching for lost children. Those who do so face the extra difficulties of not having access to information or agency assistance, but as the following account by a birth mother called Julie shows, if there is a will, there is sometimes a way.

'I was forced to part with my son when he was six weeks old but he was never out of my mind. When I married six years later I told my husband. There the secret remained for twenty-two years but after watching a TV programme on adoption I realised that this was 1990 and it was no longer a terrible thing to have an illegitimate child. I desperately wanted to find him to tell him my side of the story – that I didn't give him up out of choice. Also I was burning with curiosity to know whether he was alive or dead.

'You can't imagine the terrible way I was treated. I had doors closed in my face, letters went unac-

knowledged, and Social Services had me in tears. But once I started I was not going to be beaten. Luckily for me my father had kept a note of the adoption date. I buried myself in St Catherine's House and listed all the names round the adoption date. I had to purchase twenty-nine adoption certificates before I found one which tallied with my son's birth date. Some people have taken much longer and spent much more money. I became obsessed with finding him and would have spent anything. I was planning to get a second job if I had to. Then I worked on telephone directories and electoral registers until I tracked him down.

'I found myself an intermediary who wrote my son a very clever letter asking him to ring for more information. During this time I just couldn't contain myself and went to look at his house. This was a very anxious time for me, but at last the intermediary told me that he had spoken to his parents and wanted me to ring him up.

'It was weird and wonderful speaking to this strange grown-up person who was also my son. I was so excited and asked lots of questions. We talked for ages. He was glad that I had found him and said, "God you went to all that trouble to find me." He says he was shocked when he got the letter but when he was offered counselling he said he was old enough to handle it. His parents were very good about it and said he was old enough to know what he was doing. He took the letter and showed it to everyone at work so he must have been excited.

'We arranged to meet in a hotel. Our reunion went really well and we chatted for about three hours. Both of us brought photographs and it was lovely to see what his adoptive parents looked like. He calls me Julie and that's how I sign myself in my letters. Now I can't wait for him to meet the rest of my family. My father says it is his dearest wish to meet his first grandchild.

'I want to know everything about him but I am aware that I must proceed cautiously. He's very busy making his own life and I am the one who makes the phone calls. He doesn't seem as eager to meet my children as they are to meet him. He has an adopted sister to whom he is very attached. I think this is a problem for him because she's adopted too and he doesn't know how she will feel about her own mother. I've been reading a lot and when he comes here I'm not going to swamp him with family. I was hoping he would come for Christmas but my husband pointed out that he's been with his family every Christmas for twenty-two years and that's how it will still be. Just the same, what I am looking forward to the most is being able to buy him presents.

'Another reason why I mustn't go overboard is for the sake of my family. My husband and children all had a hand in helping at St Catherine's House but my husband has had twinges of jealousy and one of my sons did accuse me of being able to think of nothing else.

'Finding my son has done so much for my self-confidence. I have always suffered from depression

which my husband said was to do with the adop-
tion. I am a nervous person and was even panicky
about travelling. The fight to find my son has made
me brave. I had to travel; I had to learn how to
use documents. My greatest satisfaction is that I've
beaten the system.'

When birth parents seek out their children they take
the risk of being rejected. Adoptive parents can be so
difficult that adoptees sometimes cannot cope with
divided loyalties. Or young adults can be too confused,
angry and unsettled to want a reunion. It is therefore
very important to try and choose the right time for an
approach. In Julie's case it proved a good time to find
her son. At twenty-two he was independent enough to
decide whether he wanted to be contacted or not. It
would not be right for a birth mother to appear on the
scene before her child is eighteen. Just as many experts
feel that eighteen is a vulnerable age to start searching,
so it is a vulnerable age to be found. Even if adoptees
turn birth parents away, the attempt can have a positive
aspect. For some mothers the image of the baby they
gave up for adoption years earlier gets fixed in their
minds. A meeting gives them a more realistic picture of
the person that that baby has grown into. They also
stop waiting for the telephone call or message that never
comes.

I was greatly struck in my interviews by the delight
most people took in their newly-found half- or full
brothers and sisters, especially if they had been only
children. Relationships between them can develop more
easily and often turn out to be more enduring and

satisfying than those with the parents. This is because they are nearer in age and have more in common, and they do not have the same legacy of guilt or resentment. Sometimes the sibling becomes a substitute for a parent. Clare, who gave such a harrowing account of uncovering her mother's suicide, had a marvellous reunion with her older sister whom she discovered by advertising in the local newspaper.

'When she telephoned me she told me she had always known about me and had wanted to find me. I started to cry because I felt wanted. I was wanted. Impulsive as usual I said I was driving straight down. My boyfriend dropped everything and came too. He's so good, puts up with everything. We slept outside the house. I was so nervous I couldn't sleep. I was just jiffling away in the car. When the light came up my sister's husband took us in for breakfast. My sister hadn't come down yet so he gave me a photo and my heart was beating because she looked so lovely. She looked a little bit like me in the face. I can't remember the colour of her eyes, not having grown up with it. She came down and we crossed to each other and hugged. I was blubbering like anything. She got out the photos and I saw the first pictures of Mum. There I was on the threshold of meeting real relatives – not pretend ones like I'd had all my life – the sort of people I had called auntie – and they were mushrooming by the minute. My adoptive mother has been faultless about it. She said to a neighbour, "All in all I'm glad because she's got someone if *something happens to me." It's a funny thing to say but I think I could get married now because I'd have family of my own on my side of the church.'*

The sort of problems that can arise between reunited brothers and sisters also arise in step-families. There is the potential incestuous problem described above, if siblings find themselves physically attracted to each other. Adoptees who find they have full siblings naturally feel upset and resentful at having been left out. There can also be much jostling for the mother's attention, and jealousies can get stirred up. But the tensions caused by feelings of jealousy and loyalty happen in every family and can be resolved if people are sensitive to each other.

A real dilemma can arise if a birth mother does not allow an adoptee to meet brothers or sisters. Does she have a right to keep her children apart? Gary Kitson, who has spoken publicly on this matter, found himself in this situation when his mother, whom he found after a laborious search, refused to see him. Her views were relayed to him in a solicitor's letter: 'We are instructed that the disclosure of your birth would cause not only distress to her but other members of her family.' It might be wiser for Gary to respect his mother's wishes, but he feels she has no moral right to stop him approaching his half-sister.

What these very personal accounts have shown me is that people who are involved in reunions need to negotiate the level of contact. It really helps to proceed cautiously and not rush in with preconceived ideas about roles and status. For most people reunions are not the end of the search but the beginning of evolving relationships, and, like all relationships, especially those in step-families, need to be worked out over a period of time so that they become comfortable for everyone.

THE FUTURE

It must be obvious by now that I am on the side of openness in every aspect of adoption (though I feel it is too early to form a judgement about open adoption in its extreme form as practised in some private adoption arrangements in the USA). Yet I did not start out with this as a preconceived idea and have been won over by research and anecdotal evidence. Even if it is not always put into practice, a more open spirit in adoption has now been generally accepted and will be reflected in changes to the adoption law proposed for 1992. At the time of writing, a government review of adoption practice is being undertaken. The first paper discusses ways in which birth parents could be given greater involvement in the selection of adopters, and questions the practice of severing links with the birth family after adoption. What form the legislative changes will take is not yet clear but the preferred approach seems to be for a more flexible 'menu' approach to take into account the needs of children in various adoption circumstances. Such changes would effectively make searching redundant. Adoptees would either have enough information to satisfy them, or would be able to establish some form of contact with the birth family without difficulty.

Unfortunately, just as one battle against secrecy has been waged and more or less won, another is threatening in the area of artificial reproduction. Adoption experts are very concerned that the lessons so painfully learnt in their field are being ignored by those involved in creating children through medical means. They argue that children who have artificial genetic histories have the same need and right to know about their origins as adopted children. In order to understand the link (which is often denied) with the adoptive experience, it is necessary to distinguish between the different forms of artificial reproduction.

Artificial insemination is the placing of a sperm inside a woman's vagina or womb by a medical technique rather than by intercourse. The sperm can be the husband's or partner's (AIH) or a donor's (AID) if the husband is sterile. There are no problems regarding imparting information to a child born by AIH – that is with the full complement of both parents' genes. The child is the child of its parents in every sense, and just needed a technical boost to get it on its way. But what about a child produced by donor insemination (DI) who has genes from the mother combined with genes from a donor? Approximately 1,700 children a year are born in the UK as a result of DI.

The situation at present is that the child, who is brought to term in a natural pregnancy, is legally the child of the mother and her husband or partner. There is nothing on the child's birth certificate to indicate that there was a different biological father. The anonymity of the donor is guaranteed by law so unless this child is told the truth about its origin by the parents, it need never know.

Adoption experts are not critical of artificial insemination in itself, which gives hope to thousands of infertile couples. They are concerned about the secrecy, enshrined in law, around the issue of information. If the parents do not elect to tell the child how it was conceived – and many doctors advise them not to – that child will be for ever ignorant. Knowing what they now know about the psychological necessity of genetic information to adoptees, these experts are worried about the effects of secrecy on children born through donor insemination. The 1990 Human Fertilisation and Embryology Bill went some way to meeting these worries by requiring the Licensing Authority, set up by the bill, to keep information about donors and to regulate certain circumstances in which information may be disclosed. A person aged eighteen or over may, on application, be given certain non-identifying information about the donor. Certain information may also be provided to a person under eighteen who proposes to marry. But the only people who will apply for this information will be those children who have found out, or been told that they have a different father from the one who brought them up. And what if the rudimentary and non-identifying information they receive does not satisfy them? What if, like many adoptees, they become obsessed with knowing or meeting their biological fathers? Will we have difficult and traumatic searches all over again, as is happening in the United States where the children of donors are forming pressure groups and articulating their right to know?

In-vitro fertilisation (IVF) is the technique whereby a ripe egg is taken from the ovary and mixed with sperm in a dish (*in vitro*) for fertilisation. When the fertilised embryo starts to develop it is placed in the womb. IVF poses no problem as far as information is concerned when the egg comes from the mother and is fertilised by sperm from the father. Difficulties arise if the mother was infertile and the egg was taken from another woman and fertilised by the father (in which case the child has half its parents' genes), or if donors provided the embryo (in which case the child contains none of its parents' genes). A woman who brings an embryo to term is regarded as the mother even if the child is genetically not hers. It is estimated that since 1978 over 1,200 births in the UK have involved IVF.

Surrogacy occurs when one woman carries a baby to term for another with the intention of handing it over at birth. In Britain after the furore aroused by the Baby Cotton case (in which surrogate mother Kim Cotton was paid to be artificially inseminated with the sperm of a man whose wife was unable to carry a child) the Surrogacy Arrangements Act was passed in 1985, making it illegal for a third party to take part in a commercial surrogacy arrangement. If surrogacy does take place the baby is deemed to be the offspring of the surrogate (and her husband if she is married), and the commissioning couple have to adopt the baby. In 1990 the British Medical Association reversed its ruling that doctors should not participate in any surrogacy arrangements but requests are treated with great care and caution. Nevertheless, informal surrogacy does take place though it is not known to what extent. Because the law is clear, it is to be hoped that the sort of sensational legal tussles that have hit the headlines in the USA will never occur here. The complications inherent in surrogacy can be horrendous and it is worth sparing a thought for the child who in an extreme case could technically (though not legally) have five parents – the biological parents who donated the embryo, the surrogate mother who carried it, and the social parents who adopt the child. Examples like the Baby M case in the United States, when the surrogate mother unsuccessfully fought to keep the baby she had carried, continue to raise ethical questions about whether it is right to create children with the deliberate intention of separating them from their birth mothers.

In a nutshell, the similarity between artificial reproduction and adoption is this: the child is reared by parents, one or both of whom are not the genetic parents, who can withhold this information if they so choose. Robert and Elizabeth Snowden, Christine Walby and others who have written on this subject advocate openness as an alternative to the secrecy and deceit which presently surrounds DI and IVF. The main obstacle to openness is in the 'telling'. If adoptive parents find it difficult to provide their children with satisfying information about their origins, how much more difficult it will be for parents to explain about test-tubes. But the Americans are already tackling this problem: for those involved in the field, the question is no longer *whether* to tell children how they came into the world, but *how* to tell them. Books like Lois Ruskai Melina's *Making Sense of Adoption* gives guidance to parents on the sort of conversations they can have with their children from an early age about adoption, DI, surrogacy and IVF.

In this country we are still at the stage of debating whether such conversations should be taking place at all. Doctors and counsellors who advise couples not to tell, or to tell only if they want to, believe that secrecy is in the best interests of everyone involved. They think that telling children, for instance, that they were conceived in a test-tube, or that half their genes belong to an unknown donor, would lead to insecurities and problems. They also argue that there is little likelihood of the children finding out, so why complicate matters? Since the children are loved and wanted, why risk destabilising them with irrelevant technical details? If they assume one set of origins, the fact that they are mistaken about these origins is not important. By keeping such information 'secret parents are also protected from the stigma of infertility.

Parents themselves appear by and large to subscribe to these views. In a study published in 1983 on couples who had given birth to DI children between 1977 and 1980, Snowden, Mitchell and Snowden found that the vast majority had not told and did not intend to tell their children. These parents felt that keeping a secret was a practical possibility and preferred to see it as privacy rather than secrecy. The secret was often kept so as to protect the infertile husband, or grandparents who would find it difficult to understand. Some people told partial lies, admitting to DI but pretending it was the husband's sperm. They were also understandably anxious to avoid being labelled as different or abnormal. They were concerned that disclosure might unbalance family relationships if it was known that the child was related by blood to only one side of the family. There was also a very understandable fear that if the child became aware that he or she was conceived by donor insemination, the child's relationship with the father might be damaged. Although many of them had told family and friends, this did not affect their decision not to tell their child. Some couples thought they would tell if unusual circumstances cropped up.

Those who argue for openness and honesty in these tricky and delicate situations take the line that it is almost impossible to keep a secret in a family. Someone sooner or later blurts out something. One not unreasonable scenario in this age of frequent divorce could be in the course of a marital row or break-up when an angry spouse might say, 'Well it's not my child anyway.' Also a secret has a way of growing more complicated over time. The longer it is kept, the harder it is to reveal. Sometimes if parents feel forced to disclose information much later on for medical or other reasons, it can come as a terrible shock to the child who might feel, as is frequently the case in late disclosure in adoption, that his whole life had been built on a deception. It is surely preferable that children should be told in a loving and caring way by their parents than that they should learn about it carelessly from someone else, or out of the blue at a much later stage.

In their research the Snowdens found that over half the couples they interviewed had told selected relatives and friends, all of whom had been understanding and supportive. In their book *The Gift Of a Child* they write that one disadvantage of secrecy is that it 'restricts the availability of information to new couples who could benefit from learning of the experience of others. If couples keep the whole thing secret, new couples imagine that they are unique cases and, in their isolation, they may feel even more wretched.' The more that is known about infertility the better it will be because so much of the stigma associated with it is due to a common misconception that infertility is the same as impotency.

Who is actually being protected by not telling; is it the parents or the children? Knowing what we do about adoption, should we be ignoring the rights and needs of children to information about their complicated genetic origins? It is easy to make-believe when babies are small and cuddly, but these babies grow into adolescents and then adults with distinct identities. What about their right to know? Elizabeth Snowden puts it like this:

'To set out not talking about this area is bad for family relationships. If a couple has made this choice but feels it is unmentionable then they ought to have another think about it. But I don't think it is too awful to talk about. For people who want to bring their children up with values of honesty and integrity it could be more awful not telling. Everyone knows about DI nowadays. It often crops up in the media. Just as many growing children ask their parents, "Am I adopted?" it is not difficult to imagine them asking, "Am I a test-tube baby?" They will soon notice if there are areas not being talked about and become suspicious if *they know their parents didn't have them for six or seven years. I know some families who have adopted children who have been told they are adopted and DI children who haven't been told. That can't be the right way for a family to go about it. I believe that you get a deeper experience of life if you tell the truth.'*

According to the Snowdens, the little information they have gleaned about children who were told has been positive. 'These young people had certainly been surprised when they were told, but some of that surprise was because their parents had felt the need to keep the matter such a close secret for so many years. None of them regretted the fact that their parents had had them by AID. They were enjoying life and happy to be alive and realised that they owed their existence to AID.' Research in the USA has revealed that some DI children had grown up feeling instinctively different with a strong sense of not fitting in. Learning the truth about their genetic origins gave them a tremendous sense of relief and liberation.

Despite the fears about secrecy expressed above, it is only fair to point out that social attitudes have been changing fast in the last ten years. Since Doctors Edwards and Steptoe produced the first test-tube baby in July 1978 the public has become much more aware of infertility techniques and results. Some hospitals even publicise reunion birthday parties for their IVF babies. There has been progress on the legal front too. As we have seen, the Human Fertilisation and Embryology Bill allows a person of eighteen to apply for non-identifying information about the donor. The Licensing Authority is in the process of drawing up a code of practice which will include guidance regarding the importance of the welfare of children born as a result of treatment services. It will also be necessary to make a regulation limiting the number of times the sperm or eggs of the same donors can be used. Although the chance of siblings or half-siblings meeting or marrying is unlikely, it is obviously essential that the number of pregnancies from any one donor be restricted by law.

But there is still a long way to go if the child's right to information about its genetic origins is to be fully acknowledged. There is no legal requirement for parents to tell their children, and, at the moment there is little to tell – the amount of information given to the parents about an anonymous donor is minimal. All that is usually known about him is that he is healthy, fertile, and of a broadly similar physical appearance to the husband.

There are strong arguments for keeping the donor anonymous, not least being the fear that donations will discontinue if the anonymity is removed. But the adoption experience shows that even if the information was non-identifying it would be helpful to both parents and children if it included fuller biographical details, such as talents, aptitudes and family history. Those who argue for anonymity to be removed believe that it would not only help children but would be of benefit to donors themselves who would have to think more carefully about the consequences of what they were doing. It is feared that some of them will have regrets in later life at having propagated unknown children when they were young.

Openness seems more terrifying to contemplate than secrecy, yet adoption experience has shown how vital it is for adoptees to be able to talk openly and honestly to their parents about their origins. There is no reason to believe that children born through DI or IVF will feel differently. It will be tricky to know how much to tell, when and how, but as experience is built up, guidelines from counsellors and social workers will become more freely available. It seems hard to believe now in the media's hysterical reaction to the 1975 change in law which allowed adoptees access to their original birth certificates. The predicted blackmail and legal reprisals did not take place. Adopted people have acted responsibly and with discretion. There is no reason to believe that donor children will not act as responsibly if they are given greater access to information.

THE END

I have to bring this book to an end in the knowledge that there is no end for those involved in the adoption triangle. Adoption is a life-long process of evolving relationships. When adoptive parents take on someone else's child they inevitably carry an awareness of that child's parents somewhere in their conscious or subconscious selves. The birth parents, in particular the mother, never forget the relinquished child. The child grows up with the knowledge that there are other parents out there somewhere. Searching and reunions give substance to the fantasies about the missing people in their lives.

There are some 'dos' and 'don'ts' to bear in mind when searching and uniting, but there is no substitute for understanding and compassion. If everyone in the triangle is aware of the fears and needs of the others, then the outcome can be positive. My hope is that readers of this book will learn from the moving experiences related above that adoptees do not have to feel guilty; adopters do not have to feel threatened; and birth parents do not have to be afraid.

FURTHER READING

Austin J. (editor), *Adoption: The Inside Story*, Barn Owl Books (1987).

Haimes E. & Timms, N., *Adoption, Identity and Social Policy*, Gower (1985).

Krementz J., *How it Feels to be Adopted*, Knopf, New York (1988).

Lifton B. J., *Lost and Found: The Adoption Experience*, Harper & Row, New York (1988).

Melina L. R., *Making Sense of Adoption: A Parent's Guide*, Harper & Row, New York (1989).

PAC Discussion Papers, 'Working with Mothers who Lost a Child'; 'Groups for Women who have Parted with a Child for Adoption'.

Rockel J. & Ryburn M., *Adoption Today: Change and Choice in New Zealand*, Heinemann Reed, Auckland, New Zealand (1988).

Rowe R., *Yours by Choice: A Guide for Adoptive Parents*, Routledge & Kegan Paul (1982).

Snowden R. and Snowden E. M., *The Gift of a Child*, Allen & Unwin (1984).

Snowden R., Mitchell G. D., & Snowden E. M., *Artificial Reproduction: A Social Investigation*, Allen & Unwin (1983).

Walby C. & Symons B., *Who Am I? Identity, Adoption and Human Fertilisation*, BAAF (1990).

Winkler R. & Van Keppel M., *Relinquishing Mothers in Adoption: Their Long-term Adjustment*, Institute of Family Studies, Melbourne (1984).

USEFUL ADDRESSES

Ariel Bruce Associates, 6 Regent Square, London WC1H 8HZ Tel: 071 833 2969

British Agencies for Adoption and Fostering (BAAF), 11 Southwark Street, London, SE1 1RQ Tel: 071 407 8800

British Pregnancy Advisory Service (BPAS), Austy Manor, Wootton Wawen, Solihull, West Midlands, B95 6BX Tel: 0564 793225

Family Care, 21 Castle Street, Edinburgh, EH2 3DN Tel: 031 225 6441

Family Planning Association, 27 Mortimer Street, London, W1N 7RJ Tel: 071 636 7866

General Register Office, St Catherine's House, 10 Kingsway, London, WC2B 6JP

General Register Office (CA Section), Titchfield, Fareham, Hampshire, PO15 5RR

General Register Office, New Register House, Edinburgh, EH1 3YT

General Register Office, Oxford House, 49–55 Chichester Street, Belfast, BT1 4HL

In Touch Register, 14 Ladysmith Road, Didsbury, Manchester, M20 0HL

Migrant Trust, 8 Musters Road, West Bridgeford, Nottingham, NG2 7AQ Tel: 0602 819865

The National Association for the Childless (NAC), 318 Summer Lane, Birmingham, B19 3RL Tel: 021 359 4887

Natural Parents' Support Group (NPSG), 3 Aldergrove, Normanton, West Yorkshire, WF6 1LF Tel: 0924 894 076

The National Organisation for the Counselling of Adoptees and Parents (NORCAP), 3 New High Street, Headington, Oxford, OX3 7AJ Tel: 0865 750554

Parent to Parent Information on Adoption Services (PPIAS), Lower Boddington, Daventry, Northamptonshire, NN11 6YB Tel: 0327 60295

Post-Adoption Centre (PAC), Interchange Building, 15 Wilkin Street, London, NW5 3NG Tel: 071 284 0555

Transatlantic Children's Enterprise (TRACE), Sophia Byrne, 11 St Tewdricks Place, Mathern, Nr Chepstow, Gwent, NP6 6JW

The Triangle, 8 Musters Road, West Bridgeford, Nottingham, NG2 7AQ Tel: 0602 819865

A NOTE ON THE AUTHOR

Julia Tugendhat is a family therapist and is the author of *What Children Can Tell Us About Divorce*. She has written eleven books for children and lives in London with her husband and two sons.